BEING A
TERRIFIC TEEN
IN TROUBLED
TIMES

BEING A
TERRIFIC TEEN
IN TROUBLED TIMES

ALLAN K. BURGESS
MAX H. MOLGARD

BOOKCRAFT

Salt Lake City, Utah

Library of Congress Catalog Card Number: 93-74744
ISBN 0-88494-917-6

First Printing, 1994

Printed in the United States of America

Contents

Introduction:
Sleeping in a Garage Doesn't Make You a Car

Someone once said that "sitting in church doesn't make you a Christian, any more than sleeping in a garage makes you a car." We will never become true Christians until we desire it enough to make spiritual commitments in our lives. That is what this book is all about. It has one basic purpose—to help you reach your spiritual goals.

The very fact that you are reading this book indicates that you want to live the gospel and become a more spiritual person; therefore we will not preach to you or try to convince you that the Church and the gospel are true. Rather, we will talk with you as friends and share with you some ideas that may help you live a better life and gain the strength to overcome many of the problems facing young people today.

We know that it will still be up to you to apply these principles in your life, but we want you to remember that you are never alone. As you open your heart and make an effort to live the gospel, you will be surprised by the amount of help you will receive from the Lord. Your quest for eternal life was never meant to be a solo journey, and the Lord will be with you every step of the way.

1

Becoming Celestial Is Up to You

Know this, that ev'ry soul is free
To choose his life and what he'll be;
For this eternal truth is giv'n:
That God will force no man to heav'n.

He'll call, persuade, direct aright,
And bless with wisdom, love, and light,
In nameless ways be good and kind,
But never force the human mind.
("Know This, That Every Soul Is Free,"
Hymns, no. 240.)

"I'll Starve to Death Before I Eat That Soup!"

When Allan was five years old, his dad, who was a first-class army cook, made a big pot of homemade vegetable soup. As Allan smelled it cooking, he decided that he didn't like it, even though he hadn't tasted it. After the prayer on the food had been given, Allan refused to eat the soup, saying that he wanted something else. His father told him that he would not get anything else to eat until he had eaten his soup. Allan made up his mind that he would never eat that soup—and he got nothing for supper.

When he got up the next morning, his mother made him his favorite breakfast and told him that as soon as he ate his soup he could have some. Because Allan still refused to eat the soup, he got nothing for breakfast—or lunch. When dinnertime rolled around, he was mighty hungry, and his mother made a beautiful banana cream pie for dessert. When the family sat down to eat, that same ugly bowl of vegetable soup was placed in front of Allan. Although his dad had been very patient up to this time, when Allan said that he would starve to death before he ate the vegetable soup, his dad decided it was time for action. He told Allan that he had two choices: He could eat the soup, or he could get a spanking and eat the soup. "Either way," Dad said, "you will eat that soup!"

Allan chose plan B, which was to get spanked and then eat the soup. After his spanking he decided that maybe he would try the soup. He took one bite and spit it onto the kitchen floor. His dad took him into the next room, spanked him for spitting, and explained to him that if he spit again he would be spanked again. Allan wisely decided that he would eat his soup. And he did—about three spoonfuls, with the help of his dad.

Allan then got to eat a delicious supper and to have a huge piece of banana cream pie. Allan has always liked banana cream pie, but it was years before he ate vegetable soup again. Now he eats it all the time, because he wants to.

It is always easier and more pleasant to do something when we want to do it, and living the gospel is no exception. When we start living the gospel for ourselves and not just for our parents or for someone else, we begin to grow spiritually and receive the rewards that come from obedience to God. In fact, until we start living the gospel because we want to, our spiritual growth is severely limited.

One of the greatest truths of the gospel is that spiritual growth cannot be forced. A war was fought in heaven to maintain our right to choose for ourselves. The reason for this is that love, kindness, mercy, forgiveness, and all of the other celestial traits that we came here to develop can grow only in a climate of love and freedom of choice. Because of this, we will never develop a testimony or increase our faith until we want to. If we are going to church or keeping the Word of Wisdom or paying tithing just because our parents or others want us to, we are losing out on many of the blessings that could be ours and limiting our spiritual growth.

The Commandments Are Not a Test

Undoubtedly one reason why we desired to come to earth is that in our premortal state we saw how happy our celestial parents were and we wanted to become like them. The gospel of Jesus Christ is the way to happiness. The world is filled with people who are not happy, because they are disregarding the commandments of God and are seeking happiness in some other way. All you have to do is look around you to see that this is true.

Understanding the purpose of God's commandments makes it much easier to live them. Some people seem to have the idea that God invented the commandments and that these divine laws have little to do with real life. Others think the commandments are restrictions that keep us from having any fun. There are even people who feel that God deliberately made the commandments difficult as a test to find out who is worthy of a greater glory.

The truth is that God has come to understand which laws and actions bring happiness, and he tries to teach us what these truths are. The commandments are not things we have to do so that God will want to bless us; they are eternal laws that will bless our lives as we live them willingly and completely. When we forgive others we are happier than when we hold a grudge—not just because God said so but because forgiveness is an eternal principle that leads to happiness. All of the commandments work this same way. The gospel is the great plan of happiness, and God shares it with us because we are his children.

"I Stand at the Door, and Knock"

Even though God is working full-time in our behalf, we cannot receive the blessings that he desires to give us unless we cooperate with him. Jesus said, "I stand at the door, and knock: if any man hear my voice, and open the door, I will come in to him, and will sup with him, and he with me" (Revelation 3:20). Since the door to our hearts can be opened only by us, it is we who must invite the blessings of the Lord and accept responsibility for the speed of our spiritual growth. We can crack open the door just a few inches, or we can decide to cooperate fully with God and open our hearts completely to his will and direction.

Elder Boyd K. Packer described the day when he opened his heart to God: "I went before Him and in essence said, 'I'm not neutral, and You can do with me what You want. If You need my vote, it's there. I don't care what You do with me, and You don't have to take anything from me because I give it to You—everything, all I own, all I am.' And that makes the difference." (*"That All May Be Edified"* [Salt Lake City: Bookcraft, 1982], p. 272.)

Cooperating with God really does make the difference. It takes a lot of trust to turn our lives over to God, but this is the only way that we can gain all of the blessings that he has prepared for us. We can turn ourselves over to him a little at a time or all at once, but the faster we allow God to be the captain of our souls, the faster we gain the blessings that we need.

Church Attendance Alone Is Not Enough

In 1984, the Church completed a study among young men twelve to eighteen years of age. The study tried to determine what things helped young men become worthy to receive the Melchizedek Priesthood, serve a mission, and marry in the temple. The results of this study are very helpful, and they are just as applicable and important to young women as they are to young men.

The study measured the importance of both public and private religious behavior in the lives of young men. (Public religious behavior includes participation in church meetings and activities. Private religious behavior covers activities not measured on reports, such as personal scripture study and personal prayer.)

Researchers found that although public religious worship is important, private religious activity—including personal prayer and personal scripture study—makes a tremendous difference in the worthiness and spiritual growth of young people. Those young men who were studying the scriptures and praying on a regular basis were the ones who were worthy to serve missions, hold the priesthood, and marry in the temple. (See "Key to Strong Young Men: Gospel Commitment in the Home," *Ensign*, December 1984, pp. 66–68.)

There are at least two reasons why this is the case. First, the very fact that a young person is having personal prayer and studying the scriptures indicates that he or she has made a personal commitment to the Lord and his commandments. Second, two of the greatest sources of spiritual nourishment are prayer and scripture study.

Elder Bruce R. McConkie said that the formula for receiving personal revelation from the Holy Ghost is simple, and it is not surprising that two-thirds of his formula consists of prayer and scripture study. Here's Elder McConkie's formula: (1) Search the scriptures; (2) keep the commandments; and (3) ask in faith. (See "How to Get Personal Revelation," *New Era*, June 1980, p. 50.) In order to help you in these two important areas, the next two chapters in the book discuss things you can do to improve your personal prayers and scripture study.

Ideas to Remember

1. It is easier to live the gospel when we want to.
2. God knows and loves each of us personally, and all of his efforts are directed toward helping us return to live with him again.
3. Because God loves us, he will never ask us to do anything that is not for our best good. His commandments are simply laws and truths that, if followed, bring happiness.
4. Spiritual growth cannot be forced. We will not grow spiritually until we want to, for the attributes of God grow only in a climate of love and agency.
5. Christ desires to help us, but it is up to us to invite his teachings and power into our hearts.

6. Personal prayer and personal scripture study are vital if we desire to increase our faith and gain greater spirituality.

7. Spiritual growth follows spiritual commitments. As you read the chapters in this book, commit to the Lord that you will do your best to keep his commandments, and ask him to help you keep these commitments. Much of the strength that you need will come from your personal prayers and from sincere scripture study. Church programs, parents, teachers, and good friends will also help you fulfill your goals.

2

Joining the Search

As I search the holy scriptures,
Help me ponder and obey.
In thy word is life eternal;
May thy light show me the way.
(C. Marianne Johnson Fisher,
"As I Search the Holy Scriptures,"
Hymns, no. 277.)

There's No Better Late-Night Snack

A few years ago a restaurant printed up place mats that gave silly reasons why everyone liked this restaurant's chicken. The authors enjoyed reading these place mats so much that we decided to think up twenty reasons why people love the scriptures. Some of the reasons are on the light side, but unlike those on the place mats, most of these reasons are true. As you read through this list, see how many of the reasons match your feelings concerning the scriptures.

1. They help us answer our problems.
2. They are ready to travel on a moment's notice.
3. They increase our love and wisdom.
4. They are user-friendly.
5. There's no better late-night snack.
6. They lead us to do right.
7. They are more fun than homework.
8. They fit anyone's schedule.
9. They help us feel peace, joy, and happiness.
10. They are easy to get along with.
11. They can bring peace to our hearts.
12. They get along with kids.
13. They are fun to share.
14. They are great company on a trip.
15. They increase our desire to do right.
16. You don't have to dress up to enjoy them.
17. They don't snore.

18. They help us to love people more.
19. They don't hog the covers.
20. They love you just the way you are.

Some people think of scripture study as something they *have* to do, not something they *want* to do. Since most people desire blessings from God, these reluctant scripture readers must not be aware of the many blessings—including those listed above—that they can receive from scripture study. The scriptures and the writings of the latter-day prophets are filled with promises to those who study the scriptures daily. Rather than try to list all of these blessings, we chose four short quotes that refer to just a few of them. As you read these quotes, see how many of the promised blessings are ones that you are striving for in your life.

Spencer W. Kimball: "I find that all I need to do to increase my love for my Maker and the gospel and the Church and my brethren is to read the scriptures. . . . I prescribe that for people who are in trouble." (*The Teachings of Spencer W. Kimball,* ed. Edward L. Kimball [Salt Lake City: Bookcraft, 1982], p. 135.)

Boyd K. Packer: "If your students are acquainted with the revelations, there is no question—personal or social or political or occupational—that need go unanswered. . . . Therein we find principles of truth that will resolve every confusion and every problem and every dilemma that will face the human family or any individual in it." (*Teach the Scriptures* [address to religious educators, 14 October 1977], p. 5.)

Bruce R. McConkie: "There's an increase in faith and a desire to do what's right and a feeling of inspiration and understanding that comes to people who study the gospel—meaning particularly the Standard Works—and who ponder the principles, that can't come in any other way" (*Church News,* 24 January 1976, p. 4).

Nephi: "Feast upon the words of Christ; for behold, the words of Christ will tell you all things that ye should do" (2 Nephi 32:3).

It is amazing to realize how many different blessings God and his servants have promised to those who faithfully study the scriptures. Since the Lord always keeps his promises, we will surely receive these blessings as we do our part. For example, Jacob said that the word of God "healeth the wounded soul" (Jacob 2:8). At one time or another, all of us suffer from spiritual and emotional wounds, such as depression, bitterness, loneliness, guilt, insecurity, and discouragement. The following story illustrates well how reading the word of God can bring the Spirit into our lives and literally heal our wounded souls.

A young man named Richard had rebelled against the teachings of his family and of the Church. He would even come home drunk, stand at his parents' bedroom door, and laugh at them. After trying everything else, his father said, "Richard, when you hit rock bottom, turn to the scriptures."

After high school Richard really went downhill. He left home, became heavily involved in drugs, and associated with friends that continued to pull him down. Finally he became so depressed that he was committed to a mental hospital and confined to a padded cell.

One day he remembered his father's words and asked for a Book of Mormon. At first he wanted to read it to prove that his father was wrong. Richard was sure that there was no way the Book of Mormon could really help him with his problems. In spite of his negative feelings, something began to happen to him. When he finished reading the book, he decided to read it again, and then again. He read the Book of Mormon seven times, and sometime during his reading he learned for himself that the Book of Mormon was true.

As his testimony developed, so did his desire and

strength to put his life back together. Richard eventually knelt at an altar in a holy temple of God and was sealed to a wonderful young woman for eternity. (From James M. Paramore, *Hold to the Rod: Scripture Motivation and Comprehension Series,* teacher's manual, lessons 4–6, p. 9.)

Richard's story demonstrates the great power that accompanies the study of the word of God. Although his experience seems fairly dramatic, it happened over the span of several years as he continued to study the scriptures. Many of the blessings that come from scripture study come gradually and quietly, but most people notice a real difference in their lives within a few weeks of starting a regular program of scripture study.

A group of teenagers who had been studying the scriptures for about eight months were asked if they had noticed much difference in their lives because of their study. All twenty-one of them indicated specific blessings that they had received. They said such things as the following: I get along better with my family; my bad habits are easier to control; I have found real happiness as I have come to know God; coupled with prayer it is the most important thing I have ever done; I now know that God loves me; I have received the strength to live the gospel.

There is overwhelming evidence that blessings really do come to those who regularly and sincerely study the scriptures. No wonder the Aaronic Priesthood survey conducted by the Church indicated that prayer and scripture study were vital to spiritual growth.

Lost for Five Days

In the fall of 1989, a ten-year-old boy named Joshua was lost in an abandoned mine. He had gone into the mine with his father, a group of Scouts, and several leaders. Somehow he got separated from the group and eventually ended up in a six-foot-wide, twenty-five-foot-deep ore cavity. He had no food or water, and no warm clothing, matches, or flashlight.

It was five days before he was found. During that time he sang songs such as "I Am a Child of God" and prayed that someone would find him.

A search involving hundreds of people took place, with special rescue teams and trained dogs searching the numerous mine shafts. Sixty-five hundred man-hours were spent in the search, and the mine was searched six times before the searchers were finally ready to call it quits and seal up the entrance.

When a high priest named John heard that they were going to seal up the mine, he had a feeling that he needed to go back there and try one last time to find Joshua. John's grandfather had been the mine superintendent, and John had explored the abandoned shafts since he was eight years old.

Meanwhile, two other Church members, Brother Guymon and Brother Christianson, had been praying for some new leads. After four days of searching, they knew that they would need the help of the Lord to find Joshua. As Brother Guymon offered a fervent prayer in his motel room that night, he received a strong impression that he should search again in a particular section of the mine.

The next day these three men looked over the maps of the old mine tunnels and began to search the area that

Brother Guymon had felt impressed to explore once again. They realized that this would probably be the last chance to find Joshua before the mine entrance was sealed. Around two o'clock in the afternoon, Brother Guymon heard a faint noise. He said that "it was a teeny, tiny noise like a little squeak." Even though he had heard a thousand noises during the past five days, it seemed as if the Spirit was telling him that this noise was important. Brother Guymon had often been kidded about his poor hearing, so he feels that the Lord helped him in this instance. The three men became completely still and heard a faint call for help. They eventually found Joshua huddled in the back of a small ore cavity, hidden from view by a load of debris. After five long days, Joshua had been found.

This story illustrates the difference between just looking and really searching. These people didn't quickly run through the mine tunnels and call it a day. They were committed to finding Joshua, no matter how long they might have to search. They also realized the importance of having the help of the Lord and responding to his Spirit.

Too often many of us simply hurry through our reading of the scriptures. Talking about the scriptures, King Benjamin taught his sons, "Ye should remember to search them diligently, that ye may profit thereby" (Mosiah 1:7). The Lord has never asked us to just *read* the scriptures. He has used such words as *study, seek,* and *search diligently.* When we search the scriptures with the same desire and energy that Joshua's rescuers put into their search, the scriptures come alive to us.

One mistake some people make is to set a goal to read a certain number of pages or chapters a day. This can lead a reader to concentrate on getting through a certain block of scripture rather than on taking the time to search for meaning and personal application. Many great concepts are lost when we hurry to finish a reading assignment, a chapter, or a book. One page searched carefully is usually much more beneficial to us than several chapters read quickly.

A better goal than reading a set number of pages or chapters is to study for a certain number of minutes each day. A time goal exerts no pressure to hurry through the scriptures. Even a general goal of searching the scriptures every day—without any specified time—can be a valuable goal. Then, depending on the specific circumstances of each day, we may search the scriptures five minutes or forty-five minutes.

It makes no sense to begin a search unless we know what we are searching for, and this certainly applies to the scriptures. There are many things we can search for, such as answers to specific questions, solutions to personal problems, insights that will help us present a lesson or talk, or guidance to help us get along better with our families.

Many times our desire is simply to know how to live a better life and draw closer to our Father in Heaven. If that is our goal, we should search for ways we can apply the things we are learning from the scriptures. We get much more out of the scriptures when our goal is to *live* more doctrine, not just to *find* more doctrine.

There is no reason to rush through the scriptures, just so we can say that we have read them. We should not feel pressure to hurry on to another verse or chapter. The real joy of scripture study comes as we slow down and take the time to look for things that will help us overcome our problems and live better lives.

Hearing the Voice of the Lord

There is more to understanding the scriptures than just consistent study. The scriptures were written under the direction of the Holy Ghost. In order to understand them, we must have that same power. The Holy Ghost can act as a special guide and teacher to help us in our study of the scriptures.

Although the Lord wants to speak to us through his scriptures, we sometimes don't hear his voice. Considering the following situation may help us to understand what we can do to become more receptive to the Spirit:

Suppose we are at a noisy and crowded airport, and we spot some of our friends. We can see that they are really excited, and they are shouting something to us. Because they seem so excited, we wonder what they are saying; but the noise and the distance are so great that we cannot hear them. What are some things we could do to hear them better and understand what they are saying?

1. Desire, of course, has to precede everything else. Unless we really want to hear, we may simply nod our heads, wave, and go on our way.
2. We could move closer to our friends.
3. We could try to find a quiet place and eliminate as much noise and distraction as possible.
4. We could put more energy into concentrating and really try to hear what they are saying.

These same four steps are things that we can do to hear the Spirit of the Lord more clearly and, therefore, to gain a deeper understanding of the scriptures.

1. *Desire.* Our first desire should be to have the Holy Ghost with us in our scripture study. This will not only help us understand the scriptures but also help us to apply them in our lives. Each time you study, it is important to ask the Lord to bless you with his Spirit.

2. *Move closer.* We move closer to the Lord by living the gospel better. This makes it possible for the Spirit to be with us as we study. When we're trying to live the teachings that we understand, the Spirit reveals new truths to us.

3. *Eliminate distractions.* The voice of the Lord is a still, small voice—a whisper. That is why it is so important to find a place and a time that allow you to study without interruption.

4. *Concentrate.* It is important to have an inner quietness, as well as an outer one. Sometimes you may be thinking so much about schoolwork, family problems, friends, and other concerns that it is difficult to concentrate on the scriptures. Beginning your scripture study with prayer can really help. The more effort you put into understanding and applying the scriptures, the more the Lord will bless you with his Spirit.

Ideas to Remember

1. Numerous blessings are promised to those who regularly and sincerely study the scriptures.

2. The Lord has never asked us to just *read* the scriptures but has used such words as *study*, *seek*, and *search diligently*.

3. A better goal than reading a set number of pages or chapters is to study for a certain number of minutes each day. This helps you to slow down and concentrate on what you are studying.

4. There are many things that you can search for in your scripture study. One of the most important is teachings that will help you to live a better life and draw closer to your Father in Heaven.

5. We get more out of the scriptures when our goal is to *live* more doctrine, not just *find* more doctrine.

6. The scriptures were written under the influence of the Holy Ghost, and we need the direction of the Holy Ghost in order to understand and apply them.

7. Four things that you can do to hear the Spirit of the Lord more clearly and, therefore, to gain a deeper understanding of the scriptures are as follows:

    A. Desire to have the Spirit with you and pray for the help of the Spirit.
    B. Move closer to the Lord by living the gospel better.
    C. Find a quiet place and eliminate distractions.
    D. Concentrate better by putting aside the concerns of the world and think about what you are studying.

3

Receiving Power Through Prayer

When thorns are strewn along my path,
And foes my feet ensnare,
My Savior to my aid will come,
If sought in secret prayer
(Hans Henry Petersen, "Secret Prayer,"
Hymns, no. 144).

"Why Not Just Pray over the Intercom?"

A few years ago, a father had the following prayer experience with his fifteen-year-old son. Because their family was going in so many different directions, they had finally decided as a family that they would have prayer together even if only two members of the family were present. One evening Dad and Brian, the teenage son, were the only ones home. When bedtime rolled around, Dad pushed the button on the intercom and asked Brian to come upstairs for prayer.

Hoping to avoid family prayer, Brian called back on the intercom and reminded his dad that no one else was home. His father responded, "That's OK. Let's you and me say one anyway."

However, Brian had not given up yet, and after a pause he told his dad that he was already in bed. Dad stood firm and told him to come upstairs and pray anyway. Brian thought for a minute and came up with a new and creative idea. He suggested that his dad say the prayer over the intercom and promised that he would listen. Brian generously declared that he would even get down on his knees while the prayer was said.

This idea seemed irreverent to Brian's father, even though he was impressed with his son's creativity. Once more he asked Brian to come upstairs, and having run out of ideas, Brian obeyed. The father prayed on their behalf, and Brian went back to his bedroom still asking why they couldn't pray over the intercom. (From Brent Barlow, "Except Ye Become as Little Children," *Deseret News*.)

Can you see any problems with Brian's attitude toward prayer? If this story paints an accurate picture of Brian's approach to all of his prayers, is it likely that his prayers will be answered? Can you think of any quotes or scriptures you have heard that suggest that we need to approach prayer seriously and sincerely in order to receive an answer? One of the most famous statements about prayer is Moroni's promise in the last chapter of the Book of Mormon. Moroni declared that if we would pray "with a sincere heart, with real intent, having faith in Christ," then our prayers would be answered (see Moroni 10:4–5).

We can kneel down and address our Father in Heaven and say a prayer, and yet not pray at all. This is because a prayer doesn't start with our lips but with our hearts. We communicate with God spirit to spirit and heart to heart. Just like anything else of value, prayer takes effort. A helpful way to improve your prayers is to imagine that it takes a lot of effort on your part to get your prayers into the air, through the ceiling, and all the way up to the celestial kingdom; a weak, half-hearted prayer just won't make it.

However, the first step in improving our prayers is a simple but important one—we need to really want to. When we have things in our lives that we want to pray about and we pray from our hearts, good things begin to happen to us. If you will read the rest of this section with a willing and prayerful heart, the Spirit can help you recognize some of the things that you can do to improve your prayers.

Getting Our Prayers past the Ceiling

We live in a world that is filled with distractions. Bishop H. Burke Peterson suggested a process we can follow to block out these distractions and improve the quality of our prayers. As authors we have taken the liberty of dividing his counsel into steps so that his ideas can be more easily identified and put into practice:

1. "Go where you can be alone, go where you can think, go where you can kneel, go where you can speak out loud to him. The bedroom, the bathroom, or the closet will do."
2. "Now, picture him in your mind's eye. Think to whom you are speaking, control your thoughts—don't let them wander, address him as your Father and your friend."
3. "Now tell him things you really feel to tell him—not trite phrases that have little meaning, but have a sincere, heartfelt conversation with him."
4. "Confide in him, ask him for forgiveness, plead with him, enjoy him, thank him, express your love to him."
5. "And then listen for his answers." ("Adversity and Prayer," *Ensign,* January 1974, p. 19.)

As we, the authors, have talked with teenagers—and also with adults—about their prayers, we have noticed some common problems or misconceptions that many of us have. As you read through this list, think about your prayers and see if any of these problems sound familiar to you.

1. *Sometimes we expect immediate answers.* The Lord has never promised us immediate answers, yet we sometimes set a deadline and expect God to keep it. For example, one person told the Lord that he would study and pray for one full week to know if the Church is true. When he didn't receive a testimony by the end of the week, he was very disappointed and discouraged. This led him to doubt that he would receive an answer at all, and he quit reading and praying. God will answer our sincere prayers, but he will do it according to his timetable. As you think about this person who quit studying and praying after one week, do you wonder how much he really wanted to receive an answer?

Spencer W. Kimball once prayed eighty-five days for strength to fulfill his responsibilities as a new Apostle, and a faithful bishop prayed for more than eight months before a particular concern was resolved. Neither of these men gave up; they prayed until they received an answer. Because of the effort they had put forth, it seems likely that the answers they received were especially rewarding.

2. *Sometimes we don't listen for an answer.* How many times have you asked someone a question and then immediately turned around and left before he or she had time to answer? Your response to this question is probably *never.* Not staying to hear the answer not only would be rude but also would show that you really didn't want an answer very much.

Sometimes we do this with the Lord—we pray and then immediately jump to our feet and get so involved in other things that when he tries to get through to us he gets a busy signal. We may think the Lord is not listening, when the real problem is that we are not listening.

This problem of being too busy to listen to the Spirit was illustrated by an experience of Bishop John Wells, a former member of the Presiding Bishopric of the Church. One of his sons was killed by a freight train and Bishop Wells's wife was overcome with grief.

One day soon after the funeral, Sister Wells was lying on her bed, still filled with anguish, when her dead son appeared to her and said, "Mother, do not mourn, do not cry. I am all right." He said that he had tried to see his father, but, as Elder Harold B. Lee explained in a 1956 talk, "he couldn't reach him. His father was so busy with the duties in his office he could not respond to his call." He said to his mother, "You tell father that all is well with me, and I want you not to mourn any more." (See Harold B. Lee, *Prayer* [address to religious educators, 6 July 1956], pp. 14–16.)

What a classic example this is of missing out on great spiritual blessings because of failure to listen. Brother Wells was so busy doing Church work that he did not have time to listen for promptings from the other side of the veil. Pondering and listening will be discussed in greater detail later in this section.

3. *Sometimes we expect our prayers to be answered without any effort on our part.* God is not a heavenly Santa Claus but a loving Father who wants us to grow. If he simply gave us the things we need without any effort on our part, we would always be spiritually dependent upon him and would never develop the spiritual muscles that we need to become like him. Therefore, he will never give us more help than we need.

But it is also important to remember that he will never give us *less* help than we need either. The scriptures tell us that God will help us do anything that he has asked us to do, and that he won't allow us to be tempted beyond our ability to resist (see 1 Nephi 3:7; 1 Corinthians 10:13).

4. *Sometimes we ask for harmful or impossible things.* For instance, one farmer may be praying for rain, while the farmer next to him has just cut his hay and is praying that it won't rain. Or, four different people may have interviewed for the same job, and each of them may ask God for help to get it.

We need to be careful that we don't ask for something

that would take away another person's agency. Martha may pray that Brett will like her and ask her to the prom, or Cory may pray that his parents will love each other again and not get a divorce. God will do his best to help people make the right decisions, but if they do not respond to his Spirit he will not try to force them to feel a certain way. He would not do this even if he could, because one of the most important principles of the gospel is our freedom to choose for ourselves.

Another potential problem with our prayers is that we don't have the vision that God has, and we sometimes ask for things that will be harmful to us or to someone else. Because God loves us, he will probably say no. When we don't receive the answer we want, we may think that God hasn't answered us at all. The truth may be that he has been kind enough to refuse our request. We have to have enough trust and confidence in him to accept his answer, whether or not it is the answer that we want.

5. *Sometimes we don't recognize answers to our prayers.* Since there are many ways that prayers may be answered, all of us struggle at times to recognize God's responses. This is especially true of those who are just beginning to pray.

Occasionally, we may receive strong and forceful answers, but most of the time answers come in a quiet way, such as a warm feeling, a feeling of peace, ideas that help us solve our problems, a voice in the mind, or feelings of assurance and confidence. Sometimes the Lord will guide us to someone else who will give us the answers that we seek.

Feelings of uneasiness, insecurity, doubt, or other negative feelings may signal negative answers to our prayers. The more we continue to pray and seek the help of our Father in Heaven, the easier it becomes to recognize his answers.

God Is Not like a Candy Machine

Located just inside the doors of most large grocery stores are several candy machines. All a person has to do is decide what he wants, place a coin in the appropriate slot, and turn the handle, and out comes the wished-for candy or toy. Some people approach prayer the same way. They think of heaven as a large supplyhouse to which they can phone in their orders and immediately get what they desire. Would you be surprised to find out that these people have very few prayers answered?

The real purpose of prayer is to be able to draw upon the great power, knowledge, and love that Heavenly Father desires to share with us. In order to do this, we need to have enough confidence in God to pray that his will, not ours, will be done. No matter how much we want something, a *no* answer can be acceptable to us if we honestly believe that the Lord knows what is best for us. When we approach God with this attitude, great things happen.

One of the most important prayers ever uttered was the prayer given by the Savior in the Garden of Gethsemane. While he was suffering for our sins, his pain became so intense that he prayed, "Father, if thou be willing, remove this cup from me: nevertheless not my will, but thine, be done" (Luke 22:42).

In spite of the suffering that the Savior was going through, our Father in Heaven loved *us* enough to say no to his Son, and he allowed Jesus to continue suffering. Because Jesus was willing to accept the will of the Father, all of the blessings of the Atonement are available to us. If we desire to partake of these blessings, then we, like the Savior, need to be willing to accept the will of the Father.

A young mother learned the hard way about the importance of accepting God's will. She had a thirteen-year-old daughter who was suffering from a life-threatening illness. When the daughter's ankles began to swell, it was a sign that her kidneys were failing. Her mother rushed her to the doctor.

After performing several tests, the doctor told the mother that it was the beginning of the end and that she should prepare herself for the death of her daughter. As soon as the mother arrived home, she went to her bedroom and made the decision that she would pray for her daughter's recovery with such fervency and faith that the Lord would grant her desire.

She pleaded with the Lord, but a voice inside her kept telling her that she should say, *Thy will be done.* The mother said, "No! No! I can't do that, because if I do, my daughter will die." Every time she knelt down to plead with the Lord, the Holy Ghost told her to say, *Thy will be done,* but she couldn't bring herself to say it.

She finally decided that she would fast until she could accept the Lord's will. After fasting and praying all day, she was able to kneel down and place the life of her daughter in the Lord's hands. The next morning her sick daughter came running into the kitchen. "Mom! Mom!" she cried. "My ankles are thin again!"

After hugging her daughter and with tears streaming down her cheeks, the mother hurried into her bedroom, fell to her knees, and thanked Heavenly Father for his great mercy. She apologized for her lack of trust in him. (See Maxine Crossley, "Thy Will Be Done," *Ensign,* January 1991, p. 59.)

It seems that the Lord had wanted to bless the daughter, but his major concern had been the spiritual health of her mother. Once the mother was able to change her attitude and pray in faith and trust, the Lord performed his quiet miracle. God actually helped two people that day—one physically and the other spiritually.

Ideas to Remember

1. Prayer doesn't start with our lips but with our hearts. We communicate with God spirit to spirit and heart to heart, so it is important to pray with real intent.
2. Just like anything else of value, prayer takes effort.
3. Our prayers will be more effective if we go where we can be alone, picture our Father in our minds, control our thoughts, tell our Father how we really feel, enjoy his company, and listen for answers.
4. It is helpful to remember that God does not promise immediate answers. His timetable is different from ours.
5. Because God loves us, he will sometimes say no.
6. We may occasionally receive strong and forceful answers, but answers usually come as quiet thoughts or feelings.
7. Heaven is not a large supplyhouse to which we can phone in our orders and immediately receive what we desire. It is important to develop the attitude that Jesus had: Not my will, but thine, be done.

4

The Gift of Good Friends

What greater gift dost thou bestow,
What greater goodness can we know
Than Christ-like friends, whose gentle ways
Strengthen our faith, enrich our days
(Karen Lynn Davidson, "Each Life That
Touches Ours for Good," *Hymns,* no. 293).

It's More than a Game

The 1955 World Series was one that many people will never forget. This is because of a famous catch by a man named Sandy Amoros.

The memorable game was played on 4 October 1955 at Yankee Stadium. The Brooklyn Dodgers and the New York Yankees had played to a three-game tie that forced a seventh and final game. It was in the sixth inning, with the Dodgers leading 2–0, that Yogi Berra of the New York Yankees came to the plate. Berra hit a fly ball almost to the fence but was ruled *out* when Sandy Amoros made a running catch that is considered one of the best in World Series history. This catch started a double play that preserved the Dodgers' lead and eventually won them the game and the World Series. It was the Dodgers' only title in nine World Series appearances before they moved to Los Angeles.

After leaving baseball, Sandy Amoros became ill with diabetes and battled circulatory problems that ravaged his body and led to the amputation of one of his legs. Sandy's poor health and mounting medical bills left him with very little money. Before his death on 27 June 1992, many of Sandy's friends spent a lot of time raising money for his medical expenses. Among those who helped were oldtime Brooklyn Dodgers fans, Dodgers teammates—and Yogi Berra. Yes, Yogi Berra, the very man whom Sandy had caught out in the World Series.

It's plain to see that Yogi understood that friendship is

more important than a game. True friendship is different from the friendship the world teaches. The world teaches a false kind of friendship that is conditional. There are strings attached. A false friend says, "If you do something for me, then I will be your friend and love you. If you don't, then I guess we can no longer be friends." This kind of friendship is nothing more than a game, with winners and losers.

In real, unconditional friendships there are only winners. In the 1955 World Series, Sandy Amoros was the winner and Yogi Berra was the loser. In the "Eternal Series," both Sandy and Yogi were winners. Sandy won as the receiver, and Yogi as the giver.

"Not Until Tonight . . ."

Monica and Diane were what you might call casual friends. It wasn't that Diane hadn't tried to make their friendship deeper and more meaningful, but Monica was still skeptical. Diane was a cheerleader and could date anyone she wanted. She had a beautiful wardrobe and always looked like a fashion model. Why would Diane want to be Monica's friend? Monica was a "plain Jane" and didn't have much to offer Diane except friendship. Monica felt that someone of Diane's caliber must be looking for something more. She didn't trust Diane's friendship, and she wondered what was under the apparent niceness of Diane's smile.

One Friday night both girls found themselves at a party hosted by a mutual friend. After the party both Monica and Diane were out on the front lawn. Monica had heard Diane talking earlier that evening. Monica knew that she shouldn't have been eavesdropping, but she was glad that she had, for she had found out what Diane was really like.

She quietly walked up to Diane and said, "Not until tonight have I felt that you were sincere when you said that you wanted to be my friend."

Diane was surprised at Monica's remark and asked her what had happened at the party that had made the difference.

Monica explained: "I've always felt that you were my friend only on the surface. I thought you were making fun of me behind my back. But tonight I heard you stick up for Janet when the other popular girls were making fun of her. Janet isn't a fancy girl and she isn't popular, but you were her friend even when she wasn't around. I realized then that you accept people for what they are and that if you could be trusted to defend Janet when she wasn't listening, you could be trusted to be my friend."

The way we talk about other people, especially our friends, really is an indication of how much we can be trusted. Trust was mentioned often when a group of teenagers were asked what they liked in a friend. Following are some of their responses:

"A friend is someone who is willing to listen to what you have to say and listen to your problems—someone you can trust."

"You can trust them, and they will be there when you need them. Someone to talk to and share special things with. They help you and stick up for you."

"Someone who is faithful when the going gets tough and keeps by your side through thick and thin. Someone who keeps your morale up."

"Someone who I can always trust, and I know that I can talk to them any time about anything."

"They are there when you need them. They are honest. You can trust them and talk to them about personal things."

"You can share secrets with them and trust them. They respect themselves and others, and are good listeners."

As you think about trust and the role it plays in good friendships, which of the following people would you trust and confide in and really want for a friend?

1. The person who swears she will not repeat what you have told her, then tells her other friends to listen carefully the first time she reveals your secret so she won't have to *repeat* it.

2. The person who's a master at "backstabbing," attacking even those he calls his friends. You don't have any direct proof that he's been cutting *you* down, but some of the rumors you've heard have left you with a terrible backache.

3. The person who talks about others in such a way that you wish those being talked about could be there to hear the good things being said about them.

The Elevator

Ben and Scott were great buddies. They spent their summer days together, and when they weren't together they were usually talking on the phone.

One morning, bright and early, the phone rang at Scott's house. "Guess what!" Ben said excitedly. "We're getting a refrigerator!"

"Big deal. What's so exciting about that?" Scott replied. For the life of him, he couldn't imagine why Ben was so excited.

"Just look out your front window," Ben insisted, "and see the size of the box."

Scott parted the curtains and squinted against the morning sun. Then he saw it—the box. That big, wonderful box that he and Ben had been looking for. They had made plans to make an elevator just two weeks before. The plans included rope and a huge box. They had found the rope in Ben's shed and had looked for boxes behind the stores downtown, but they had finally given up. They just couldn't build an elevator without a box. And now they had one! Scott could picture the fun they were going to have, hoisting the elevator from his backyard to his balcony three floors up.

They'd have to be sneaky though. Ben's dad had heard them talking about the elevator and had told them they'd better drop that hairbrained idea.

Ben's dad thought they *had* dropped the scheme. In fact, he didn't even remember the conversation about the elevator. That's why that very afternoon he turned the box over to the boys for a hut. Ben's dad had made a club-house out of a box when he was a boy. He smiled at the boys' efforts to balance their box as they carried it to Scott's backyard.

Ben hadn't wanted to lie to his dad, but Scott had convinced him that one lie wouldn't hurt. Besides, an elevator was like a hut, and when they got through using the box for an elevator, maybe they would use it for a hut.

The perfect day arrived. There were no parents home at either Ben's house or Scott's. Another friend, Arnie, came across the street and caught them tying a rope around the box. He promised he wouldn't tell on them if they would let him help raise the elevator.

First the three friends hooked up all the ropes, and then they ran their new elevator up and down several times to make sure it worked. They even put Ben's cocker spaniel, Ralph, in the elevator and gave him a ride. They had cut out a window, and Ralph stuck his head out of it and barked all the way up to the balcony and back down to the lawn again.

Then the big moment came. It was time for the first manned elevator ride. Scott and Arnie quickly volunteered Ben to be the first to ride the elevator to the top. They said that it was only logical that he go first, since it was his parents' box to begin with. Besides, Scott and Arnie were nervous about going up in the box; of course they didn't let Ben know that.

Ben climbed into the box, and Scott and Arnie began to pull. The ascent was full of grunts and groans as the elevator teetered and swayed to the top. Just as the elevator reached the balcony, the bottom of the box gave way and Ben fell three stories to the ground. As he crashed at the bottom, his head hit a rock in the flower bed. Scott and Arnie flew down the stairs and reached Ben as he tried unsuccessfully to stagger to his feet. Each friend grabbed an arm and helped Ben to a lawn chair.

"Oh . . . my head," Ben groaned as he reached up to touch the large cut on his forehead that was pumping blood at a pretty fast pace.

"Do you think anything is broken?" asked Scott. He was thinking about how much trouble they were going to be in when his parents got home.

"I don't think so," Ben answered. "I guess I was lucky. It's a good thing you didn't mow the lawn yesterday. I kind of bounced on the long grass."

"If you're OK, we won't have to tell how it happened," said Scott. "We can just tell your dad that you tripped over Ralph and landed in the flower bed. They'll believe that, and we won't get in trouble."

When Ben's parents arrived home, the boys told them the Ralph story and Ben's parents believed it; however, a few hours later things began to unravel. Arnie started to worry that Ben might have other problems from such a high fall. Arnie fretted and stewed, and finally decided that he should tell Ben's parents what really happened.

Scott was furious. Arnie had made a promise and then he had snitched. Real friends don't snitch on each other, Scott believed, and he marched right over to Arnie's house to tell him so.

Arnie listened to Scott rant and rave. It upset Arnie that Scott was so mad, and Arnie was confused for a few minutes. But after Scott left, Arnie knew that he had done the right thing. It was all right to snitch if it meant saving a friend—even if it meant that they were all going to be in trouble.

It's obvious from this story that Scott was not a good friend. All he really cared about was himself. On the other hand, Arnie turned out to be a real friend.

Robert D. Hales described a true friend this way: "Do you know how to recognize a true friend? A real friend loves us and protects us. In recognizing a true friend we must look for two important elements in that friendship: A true friend makes it easier for us to live the gospel by being around him. Similarly, a true friend does not make us choose between his way and the Lord's way." ("The

Aaronic Priesthood: Return with Honor," *Ensign,* May 1990, p. 40.)

Good friends are like an elevator going up—they always take us safely to higher ground. Bad friends are like an elevator going down—they always take us to lower ground. Even worse, bad friends sometimes make it look as though they were taking us up, but eventually the bottom falls out and we crash.

The following comments from several teenagers indicate the importance of having friends that are like an elevator going up:

"Good friends build me up and make me feel special, important, and good. My friends help me to see the good and to live better."

"It helps me when my friends have high standards and always keep them high."

"Real friends respect me and my values. They won't pressure me into doing things that I don't feel are right. It helps me when their values are similar to mine."

Once we understand that a good friend is someone who respects our personal standards and helps us maintain them, we are in a position to make wise decisions concerning our friends. We can use the following checklist to help us to evaluate our friends and to evaluate ourselves as friends:

1. My friend doesn't ask me to do things that I feel are wrong.
2. I usually feel happy and positive when I am with my friend.
3. I notice that I behave better when I am with my friend.
4. My friend never makes fun of my personal values.
5. I feel comfortable sharing my values with my friend

and saying no when I don't feel good about doing something.

6. I never worry about getting into trouble when I'm with my friend.

Some Friendly Advice

What if someone who did not have many friends came to you and asked you what he could do? What advice would you give him? See if your advice would be similar to the following advice given by other teens:

"Don't be afraid to be friendly to people. It may seem difficult, but others also probably want to be friendly and are just afraid to."

"Look at yourself and see if you are the kind of person you would like to have as a friend. If not, change! If so, sell yourself! Say hi and smile. People warm up to these two things more than anything. Be sincere."

"Maybe the person should try to take the first step in making friends with other people and try to overcome his own inferiority complex—maybe try to make himself more presentable to others."

"They need to learn to like themselves and get comfortable with themselves. You have to talk to people in order to make friends. Smile and say hi to people. Stand up straight so that people will think that you know where you're going."

"They need to act and look as pleasant as possible and talk to other people. They need to act natural and not put up a false front."

"They need to try not to pressure everyone into doing things their way all the time."

"I would tell them to treat people how they want to be treated and tell them that listening to others is very important in having friends."

"Try to become more confident. Be more expressive. Be in good spirits, and always try to look on the bright side of things. Overlook the bad qualities of anyone you meet. Dress well and try to be clean."

"Dress neatly and look clean. Be cheerful and very friendly, but don't lower yourself or your standards in order to feel accepted."

"Be yourself! Have a nice inner-you and make a nicer outer-you so that people will want to be your friend."

"Smile and be happy. Don't talk too much. Be friendly."

"Always have a positive attitude so you are nice to have around."

"You have to be a friend in order to have one. You need to listen and sincerely care about that person. You need to treat them with the respect that you would like to receive."

Ideas to Remember

1. What goes around comes around. If you are a good friend, chances are good that you will have good friends. If you have been there for your friends when they needed someone to talk to, they will probably be there for you when you have problems. On the other hand, if you haven't put anything into your friend-ships, you probably won't get much in return.
2. Real friends make us better than we are now. Their good qualities become our good qualities.
3. True friendship has no strings attached. It is uncondi-tional love. In true friendship there are only winners.
4. When you are sinking, it doesn't work to seek help from others who are sinking. They will just drag you down with them. You need to find someone on higher ground who can throw you a rope or a life jacket.
5. Our greatest friends are Heavenly Father and Jesus. When they make a promise, they will always follow through. They are always available and will listen and help when we get into deep water. They can always be trusted. And best of all, their love is absolutely perfect.

5

Blessings Fulfilled

I am a child of God.
Rich blessings are in store;
If I but learn to do his will
I'll live with him once more.
(Naomi W. Randall, "I Am a Child
of God," *Hymns,* no. 301.)

Who Am I?

Heavenly Father has given us prophets and scriptures to let us know that we are his children. These two helps constantly remind us why we are here and what blessings Heavenly Father has for his children.

However, there is an added blessing that can be ours. It is a patriarchal blessing. Every worthy member of the Church is entitled to one of these great blessings and should prepare to receive it. President Ezra Taft Benson counseled the young women of the Church: "I would encourage you, young sisters, as you approach your teenage years, to receive a patriarchal blessing. Study it carefully and regard it as personal scripture to you—for that indeed is what it is." ("To the Young Women of the Church," *Ensign*, November 1986, p. 82.) President Benson gave similar counsel to the Aaronic Priesthood brethren (see "To the 'Youth of the Noble Birthright,'" *Ensign*, May 1986, p. 43).

By receiving a patriarchal blessing, we can more fully understand our true identity and our eternal possibilities. A patriarchal blessing can do many great things for us. President Thomas S. Monson described it this way:

> A patriarchal blessing is a revelation to the recipient, even a white line down the middle of the road, to protect, inspire, and motivate activity and righteousness. A patriarchal blessing literally contains chapters from your book of eternal possibilities. I say eternal, for just as life is eternal, so is a patriarchal blessing. What may not come to fulfillment in this life may occur in the next. We do not govern God's

timetable. ("Your Patriarchal Blessing: A Liahona of Light,"
Ensign, November 1986, p. 66.)

The early years of Lloyd's life were greatly troubled.
These were years without the gospel and its blessings.
After marrying and having children, Lloyd returned to the
Church. When he received his patriarchal blessing, he was
promised that he would work with the youth of the
Church. When Lloyd died at a relatively young age, he
had never held a Church position in which he worked
directly with young people.

Many people might wonder how this could be. What
about the promise in his patriarchal blessing? Let's consider for a moment the fact that Lloyd was involved as a
coach in many community youth athletic programs. He
had a special way of reaching out to those who were
struggling. In these outside athletic endeavors, Lloyd
helped many young people who had forgotten their identity and their possibilities.

Equally important to remember is that none of us know
how Lloyd might be helping the youth of the Church in the
spirit world. We must always remember that God's promises are given from an eternal perspective. President Monson gave us this reminder: "Patience may be required as
we watch, wait, and work for a promised blessing to be fulfilled" ("Your Patriarchal Blessing," p. 66).

We must realize that the fulfillment and understanding
of our patriarchal blessings are like the view from a train
that is going down a track at night. As the lamp on the
front of the train lights the way before us, we can see only
a few feet down the track. We must travel further down
the track to see what lies ahead. Similarly, a complete
understanding of our patriarchal blessings comes only as
we travel the tracks of eternity. We know that God will
never lie. In our patriarchal blessings, he promises us certain things. If we live worthy of those blessings, we will
see them all fulfilled.

You're Not a Loser!

It seemed that Leon had put on a football helmet as soon as he was big enough to hold his head up straight. He had two older brothers who encouraged him, and by the time they had played through high school he was totally hooked. When a community not far from his small town started a youth football program, he immediately talked his parents into signing him up to play.

The two years Leon played in this youth football program were fun and successful. He had lived on a farm away from the city, and football had given him an opportunity to meet a new group of friends. With the help of those friends, Leon had lost only two games in two years. The same group went on to play on a ninth-grade team and again enjoyed success. They were a great team, and they felt confident that they would continue to succeed.

But Leon and his teammates seemed to hit a roadblock as they began their tenth-grade year. The team got off to a bad start and lost the first two games. Practicing for the third game, they were still confident. After all, they had been a winning team for three years in a row. This year's problems were just a small setback. The team would be back in the winner's circle in no time.

They held an extra practice to put the finishing touches on their game plan and boarded the bus early the next afternoon to travel the twenty miles to the town where the next game was to be played. Leon spent most of those twenty miles thinking and talking about how the team would win the game. As the bus pulled to a stop in front of the football field, the coach stood up and began to talk to his team. In a voice that mingled discouragement with contempt, he said, "Well, we're here, but I don't know what good it's going to do us; we're just going to lose anyway. Everyone go to the lockers, get dressed, and let's get it over with."

This coach knew the great potential of his floundering team, and he thought that if he used reverse psychology, they might get mad and play a great game just to show him they could do it. But his idea backfired. His words had the effect of a pin being stuck into a balloon. Leon felt his spirits deflate, as all hope of victory left him. If the coach didn't believe his team could win, how could Leon believe it? As the team left the bus, it was obvious that they believed what the coach had just told them.

After dressing they quietly and slowly walked onto the field. Their warm-up exercises were void of fire and enthusiasm. The game was played the same way—with disastrous results. At the end of the game, Leon walked off the field with his deflated team. Their heads were down and their spirits were down. The coach was right. They were losers.

Heavenly Father has not sent us here to be losers! Only Satan would have us believe that. He might well say to us, "Well, we're here, but I don't know what good it's going to do us; we're just going to lose anyway. But get up for another day. You might as well get it over with." If we follow the path taken by Leon and his teammates, we will believe Satan's words. That belief will lead us to live our lives with our heads down and our spirits deflated—and our lives may end in disaster.

Fortunately, our patriarchal blessings can be a great counter to Satan's negative influence. Sister Elaine L. Jack posed this question: "What does a patriarchal blessing say? Have you ever heard of one which says, 'I am sorry—you're a loser. Do the best you can on earth, and we'll see you in about seventy years.' Of course not! And you never will, because of the divine qualities each of God's children has inherited. A patriarchal blessing is like a road map, a guide, directing you in your walk through life. It identifies your talents and the good things that can be yours." ("Identity of a Young Woman," *Ensign*, November 1989, p. 87.)

Each of us has been given special gifts to share with our brothers and sisters. Heavenly Father knows what those gifts are and reveals many of them to us through our patriarchal blessings. If we will remember those gifts, our confidence will increase and we will become winners time after time. Then, because we have listened to the proper coach, we will be able to look back on a life well lived and know that we are truly winners.

How Do They Know?

Louise had many concerns and had prayed earnestly for answers. She wondered if a patriarchal blessing would hold any answers and decided to take the steps to receive her blessing. As the bishop interviewed her prior to her blessing, she told him about her many problems and questions.

Her problems weighed heavily on that good bishop. He wanted to call the patriarch to make him aware of Louise's needs but decided that this would be inappropriate.

Louise fasted and prayed before going to the patriarch's home. When she arrived they spoke briefly. Then he put his hands on her head and proceeded to give her a beautiful blessing. Toward the end of the blessing, the patriarch hesitated and remained silent for a time. After this pause he continued with an inspired blessing that answered all of her questions and concerns.

Another young woman named Susan went to her patriarch with one thought foremost in her mind. Her father was not a member of the Church, and she was deeply concerned about it. She had not mentioned this to anyone, except in her prayers to Heavenly Father. The patriarch, who did not know Susan or her family situation, gave her a blessing that mentioned in detail several things concerning Susan's father and what her role would be in helping him come into the Church.

How did these patriarchs know these things? Oliver Cowdery learned the answer to this question when the Lord stated: "Yea, I tell thee, that thou mayest know that there is none else save God that knowest thy thoughts and the intents of thy heart" (D&C 6:16).

It is by revelation to God's servants—in this case, to patriarchs—that the Lord can speak to us in a very special way. We should regard these great blessings as sacred and holy. We should read them often and pray about the things declared therein. President Benson counseled the youth of the Church, "Receive your patriarchal blessing under the influence of fasting and prayer, and then read it regularly that you may know God's will for you" ("To the Young Women of the Church," p. 82; "To the 'Youth of the Noble Birthright,'" p. 44).

President Monson gave us this insight regarding the personal nature and the importance of patriarchal blessings:

> Your patriarchal blessing is yours and yours alone. It may be brief or lengthy, simple or profound. Length and language do not a patriarchal blessing make. It is the Spirit that conveys the true meaning. Your blessing is not to be folded neatly and tucked away. It is not to be framed or published. Rather, it is to be read. It is to be loved. It is to be

followed. Your patriarchal blessing will see you through the darkest night. It will guide you through life's dangers. . . .

Your patriarchal blessing is your passport to peace in this life. It is a Liahona of light to guide you unerringly to your heavenly home. ("Your Patriarchal Blessing," pp. 66, 67.)

The following experience demonstrates how much the Lord wants us to have and regularly read our patriarchal blessings. Before Debbie received her patriarchal blessing, the patriarch prepared a tape recorder so that her blessing could be recorded. The tape would be used to transcribe her blessing. However, as he started the blessing, he forgot to start the tape recorder. Debbie noticed this but decided not to disturb the spirit of the occasion. At the conclusion of the blessing, the patriarch noticed that he had not turned on the recorder. He calmly looked at Debbie and said, "I've failed to turn on the tape. Let's turn it on anyway and see what we have." As they played the tape, her entire blessing had been recorded. The Lord had made sure that Debbie had a copy of her blessing so that she could use it as a guide throughout her life.

Ideas to Remember

1. Our patriarchal blessings are given from an eternal perspective. What is not fulfilled in this life will be fulfilled in the next. As we live faithfully, time will prove that all things God has promised will come to pass.

2. Don't settle for anything less than the best. Our patriarchal blessings can give us a vision of what is truly best for us. Speaking to the young women of the Church, President Benson voiced this plea: "We have such hope for you. We have such great expectations for you. Don't settle for less than what the Lord wants you to be." ("To the Young Women of the Church," p. 84.) In a similar address to the Aaronic Priesthood brethren, President Benson said: "Live up to your godly potential. Remember who you are and the priesthood that you bear. Be modern-day sons of Helaman. Put on the whole armor of God." ("To the 'Youth of the Noble Birthright,'" p. 46.)

3. Our patriarchal blessings not only give promises but also provide counsel on things that require caution from us. We lived with Heavenly Father for a long time in the premortal life, and he knows us better than we know ourselves. He knows our weaknesses and therefore gives us counsel and advice for dealing with those weaknesses. We should carefully read and follow the counsel given us in our patriarchal blessings. In his great wisdom, the Lord knows what each of us needs to do in order to avoid the pitfalls that may lie before us.

4. It is important to have faith and hope in the Lord's promises. The opposites of faith and hope are fear and despair. As we receive and believe the things given in our patriarchal blessings, these two destructive forces of fear and despair can be dispelled from our lives.

6

Staying Morally Clean

The truths and values we embrace
Are mocked on ev'ry hand.
Yet as we listen and obey
We know we can withstand
The evils that would weaken us,
The sin that would destroy.
With faith, we hold the iron rod
And find in this our joy.
(Susan Evans McCloud, "As Zion's Youth
in Latter Days," *Hymns,* no. 256.)

The Most Important Temple on Earth

Have you ever had the opportunity to go to a sacred temple and perform baptisms for the dead? If you have, then you probably carry in your heart reverent and special feelings for the temple; even visiting the temple grounds usually brings feelings of respect and reverence. Can you imagine someone putting other people down or stealing in the temple? Would you be offended if you heard someone telling dirty jokes or swearing in the temple? Would it bother you if you found out that the temple workers went to a rest area during their breaks and watched TV shows filled with inappropriate language and scenes? Of course these things would bother many of us, because of the sacred nature of the temple. Such activities would also distress and grieve the Lord, because the temple has been dedicated to him and consecrated for his purposes.

As sacred as these temples of stone are to God and to us, there are temples that are even more important in the sight of God. Those temples are our physical bodies—the temples of our spirits. The importance of our earthly bodies was taught by Paul when he wrote, "Know ye not that ye are the temple of God, and that the Spirit of God dwelleth in you? If any man defile the temple of God, him shall God destroy; for the temple of God is holy, which temple ye are." (1 Corinthians 3:16–17.)

As we think about the sacred nature of our bodies, it becomes apparent that we need to be very careful about what we allow into our hearts and minds. The activities

described above would drive the Lord's Spirit from our
body-temples just as quickly as they would drive it from
his temple buildings.

One of the authors had the special opportunity of
attending the dedication of the Jordan River Temple with
his wife and children. Even though they were fairly
young, these children sat quietly for four hours. This is
because of the special reverence they feel for the temple.

When temples and chapels are dedicated, they are
turned over to the Lord for his purposes. When we are
baptized we do the same thing—we dedicate ourselves to
God and his purposes. We promise him that we will keep
our bodies clean and pure and dedicate our time and talents to him. As we keep our bodies clean, they become
just like temples of stone—places where the Lord's Spirit
can dwell.

The following quote is taken from the dedication of the
Spanish Fork Seminary by Elder Boyd K. Packer on 29
August 1962. As you read it, see if you can identify three
things that should take place not only in dedicated buildings but also in our lives. "In dedicating a building, we
present it officially as our gift to the Lord. . . . We are then
under serious responsibility to maintain the building as
beautiful and appealing as it can be made. We are under
responsibility to have a spirit here in the building that is
completely worthy of the ownership of the building; and
we are under the necessity of maintaining order among
the students in such a way that there will be no disrespect
either in conduct, thought, or action toward the purpose
for which this building was erected."

As we, the authors, applied this quote to our own body-
temples, we identified three things all of us can do to dedicate ourselves to the Lord: (1) We can dress and take care
of our bodies in a modest and reverent way; (2) we can
live so that the Lord's Spirit can dwell with us; and (3) we
can show respect for ourselves and for the Lord through
our conduct, thoughts, and actions.

Since points two and three are referred to throughout this book, let's zero in on point one. The issue of modesty goes much deeper than just what clothes we wear. Modesty reflects the deep respect a person has for his temple-body, for himself, and for God. Just as the buildings and grounds surrounding the temples are dressed and cared for in a way that causes people to feel greater reverence toward God, so our dress, hairstyle, and cleanliness should cause others to respect us as children of God. If the clothes you wear are too tight, too short, too low, too transparent, or too revealing—so that others think of your body more than they think of the complete you, the body-spirit-personality you—then you are cheapening the sacred temple that God has given you.

Again, modesty reflects the way we feel about the Lord and about ourselves; thus, as our testimonies grow we automatically begin to dress more modestly and give greater care to our total appearance—we begin to understand that as members of Christ's church we represent him.

Spiritual Price Tags

One of the authors went to the store with his wife to buy a toaster. Our toaster had been given to us when we were married, and it had toasted its last piece of day-old bread. We were amazed to find that there were over twenty toasters to choose from.

If you were buying a toaster, what would you look for first? Almost the first thing my wife and I did was to look at the price tag attached to each toaster. This quickly cut down our selection from twenty toasters to only two. We do have some pride, so we did not buy the cheapest toaster in the store—we bought the one that cost $1.95 more than the cheapest toaster.

Because we were willing to pay only a small amount, we ended up with a terrible toaster. It toasts bread so slowly that the bread almost turns green before it turns brown. We've considered putting the bread in the toaster just before we go to bed so it will be toasted when we get up in the morning.

Let's face it! Anything of real value has a high price attached. This pertains to spiritual things as well as to physical ones. If we want to stay morally clean, we have to pay the price.

This principle was clearly demonstrated by a young couple, Scott and Tiffany. They were deeply in love with each other and were engaged to be married. However, as their marriage day approached, they found their physical attraction to each other so strong that they feared they would lose their chastity—and their temple marriage—if they didn't change what they were doing. They had already been involved in light petting, and it was becoming more and more difficult for them to control themselves.

This is where "everything has a price" comes in. Scott and Tiffany decided that they would have to establish some personal price tags if they really desired to stay morally clean and marry in the temple. Although they wanted to be alone with each other and show their affection, they wanted moral cleanliness even more. They realized that they would have to give up some things now in order to have what they desired most; so they established two personal price tags and committed to each other that they would pay the price to protect their chastity. The price tags they decided on were (1) that they would never be in a place where they could be totally alone, and (2) that they would allow themselves only three kisses per date. They could have the kisses all at once or spread them out, but three was the limit.

As Scott and Tiffany put their plan into operation, they found it difficult to become very romantic, because as they finished a kiss one of them would say, "One down and two to go!" It was difficult at times, but because they desired virtue above everything else, they were willing to pay the price. Six weeks later they knelt at a holy temple altar, clean and pure before God.

Like Scott and Tiffany, we also need to establish personal price tags in order to maintain our chastity. Some people feel that they are different from others—that they are stronger than their physical drives. Through twenty-five years of counseling teenagers, the authors have found that no one is stronger than his or her hormones. Even General Authorities, stake presidents, and bishops have safeguards to protect them from these temptations. None of them are allowed to travel alone with a Church member of the opposite sex—not even with the Relief Society president. Heavenly Father realizes just how strong our physical drives are, and he wants us never to put ourselves in a position where these drives can take over.

Staying morally clean requires a combination of personal spiritual growth with the establishment of price tags or guidelines that can help us avoid placing ourselves in situations where we can be overcome by temptation. Here are some price tags suggested by Elder Hartman Rector, Jr., to help all of us remain morally clean:

1. Never go into a house alone with someone of the opposite sex.
2. Never, never enter a bedroom alone with someone of the opposite sex.
3. Do not neck or pet.

   4. Never park on a lonely road.
   5. Do not read pornographic literature.
   6. Do not attend R- or X-rated movies, and avoid drive-ins.
   7. Do not go to bars or gambling establishments. (See Conference Report, October 1972, p. 173.)

As you commit yourself to following these guidelines, you will greatly increase your chances of remaining morally clean. Just deciding never to park where you can be totally alone is a major step toward moral cleanliness.

Many young people will be faced with temptations that will make it necessary to establish some specific, personal price tags. Below are some examples of personal price tags that were established by several teenagers because of temptations they were facing. You can easily guess at the reasons for these particular price tags.

   1. I'll never go on another date with Jill.
   2. I'll avoid any future parties at Bob's house.
   3. I'll get out of the car as soon as we stop in the driveway, and we can do our talking on the porch.
   4. I won't watch television again with Fred in his downstairs family room, even if his parents are home.

Remaining morally clean doesn't just happen. Like all other things of worth, protecting one's purity takes planning and effort and sacrifice. The young people who set the personal price tags described above obviously feel that their virtue is worth more than a party, or a certain girlfriend, or the physical excitement that can come in the backseat of a car. These young people are holding out for the tremendous blessings that come to those who are clean. They are willing to pay the price—whatever it might be—to maintain their virtue.

"Call Back in Two Years and We'll Talk About It"

Two important "price tags" with regard to moral cleanliness have been emphasized by the Lord's prophets for many years. These two price tags are not very popular with young people who have become emotionally involved with a dating partner. They have not sought the Spirit of the Lord, or they would know that these price tags come from him. It is always a serious thing to disagree with the prophets, but it is especially serious when it can lead to the loss of one's chastity.

President Spencer W. Kimball discussed these important price tags when he said: "Any dating or pairing off in social contacts should be postponed until at least the age of 16 or older, and even then there should still be much judgment used in selections and in the seriousness. Young people should still limit the close contacts for several years, since the boy will be going on his mission when he is 19 years old. Dating and especially steady dating in the early teens is most hazardous." ("President Kimball Speaks Out on Morality," *New Era*, November 1980, p. 42.)

How do you feel about this counsel? Is this something that is difficult for you to do, or do you find these guidelines easy to follow? Those who are willing to accept the guidance of the Lord's prophets, even though it may be difficult, are demonstrating that they have the faith and commitment necessary to overcome unrighteous desires and put their trust in the Lord.

Talking again about the importance of avoiding early dating and early steady dating, President Kimball said: "The change of this one pattern of social activities of our youth would immediately eliminate a majority of the sins of our young folks; would preclude numerous, early, forced marriages; would greatly reduce school dropouts; and would be most influential in bringing a great majority of our young men and women to the holy marriage altar at the temple—clean, sweet, full of faith to become the worthy parents of the next generation." ("Save the Youth of Zion," *Improvement Era*, September 1965, p. 806.)

Why do you think President Kimball said there should be no dating *or* pairing off until at least the age of sixteen? One reason is that some young people convince themselves they are not dating, even though they pair off and spend a great deal of time with a specific member of the opposite sex. A young friend of ours was not allowed to date until she was sixteen, yet she had two babies out of wedlock by two different boyfriends before her sixteenth birthday. She and her boyfriends were constantly watching TV or going downtown or taking a walk or meeting at a dance, but they never called any of these activities *dates.* Think of the heartbreak and misery she could have avoided if she had only listened to the Lord's prophet.

God has not established these guidelines to punish us or make us miserable, but because he loves us and wants us to be happy. The Lord has asked us not to date until age sixteen and to avoid steady dating until after the young man's mission because the Lord understands our bodies and our sexual drives much better than we do.

God's great wisdom in setting these guidelines was underscored by a study conducted in the early 1980s in fifteen school districts in California, New Mexico, and Utah. The study indicated that the younger a girl is when she begins dating, the more likely it is that she will become involved sexually before marriage. The importance of following God's counsel on early and steady dating will become even clearer to you as you read the following findings from this non-Church study. Although only the statistics for young women are given, the study found that young men follow a similar pattern.

The study found that 90 percent of the girls who began dating at age twelve became involved in premarital sex. This is nine out of every ten of these girls.

Especially interesting were the study's conclusions regarding those who start dating at age fifteen versus those who wait to date until sixteen. Of those girls who started dating at age fifteen, 60 percent of them (six out of ten) lost their chastity. Of those young women who waited until sixteen to date, the percentage who lost their virtue before marriage dropped below 20 percent! This statistic is important because many young Latter-day Saints decide to start dating at age fifteen. Waiting just one more year and following the counsel of the prophets could triple their chances of staying morally clean.

Because of the significant drop in the level of sexual activity between young women dating at fifteen and those who waited until sixteen, Dr. Terrance Olson concluded: "It is apparent that there is some maturity and wisdom and sense of responsible living that a 16-year-old brings into a dating situation that a 15-year-old does not." (See Carri P. Jenkins, "Making Moral Choices," *BYU Today,* April 1985, p. 39.)

These statistics strongly support what the Lord has said; however, the best reason for waiting to date until sixteen and putting off steady dating until much later is that the Lord has asked us to follow these standards. Committing to do these things is one way that we can show our Father in Heaven that we love him and trust him.

A young man named Paul had an experience that can teach us something about early dating. When Paul turned sixteen he got up enough courage—with the help of a friend—to ask Cindy for a date. Because Paul's courage faltered at the last minute, his friend even dialed her number for him. Cindy answered the phone, and Paul asked her if she would like to go to a movie with him. At first Cindy didn't say anything; then she said that if Paul would wait a minute she would ask her dad.

Paul could hear their voices in the background, but he couldn't hear what they were saying. Finally Cindy's father came to the phone. "Paul," he asked, "don't you know that you aren't supposed to date until you're sixteen?" When Paul told him that he *was* sixteen, Cindy's father replied that Cindy was only fourteen; then he wanted to know why Paul was asking her out. Paul didn't really have a good answer, but it didn't matter, because Cindy's dad started to talk again. He said, "Why don't you call back in two years and we'll talk about it."

As you think about what Cindy's father said, it is easy to see that he really loved his daughter and wanted what was best for her. It is the same with our Heavenly Father. He cares enough for us that he has given us guidelines to ensure our safety and happiness. If someone who is younger than sixteen were to ask Heavenly Father if it is all right to go out on a date, the Lord might answer much as Cindy's earthly father did: "Why don't you call back when you're sixteen and we'll talk about it."

Ideas to Remember

1. As sacred as temples of stone are to God, our body-temples are even more important in his sight.

2. Dishonesty, dirty jokes, and crude, suggestive movies and videos are some of the things that drive the Lord's Spirit from our body-temples just as quickly as they do from his temple buildings.
3. When we are baptized we dedicate ourselves to God and his purposes.
4. Modesty reflects the deep respect a person has for his body-temple, for himself, and for God.
5. When you dress so that others think of your body more than they think of the *complete* you, you are cheapening the sacred temple that God has given you.
6. As we seek the guidance of the Lord, he will help us decide the best way to dress our sacred body-temples.
7. Everything of real value, including chastity, has a price attached. If we want to stay morally clean, we have to pay the price.
8. Each of us needs to establish personal price tags in order to maintain our chastity.
9. Two of the most important price tags are the decisions to avoid early dating and early steady dating. By avoiding these two dangerous practices, we greatly increase our chances of staying morally clean.
10. A non-Church study done in the early 1980s found that by shifting the starting age for dating from age fifteen to age sixteen, young people triple their chances of staying morally clean.
11. The best reason for waiting to date until age sixteen and putting off steady dating until much later is that the Lord has asked us to follow these standards. By doing this we show him that we love him and trust him.
12. Because Heavenly Father loves us and understands our sexual drives better than we do, he has given us guidelines that if followed, will promote our safety and happiness.

7

We Believe in Being Honest

I believe in being honest;
I believe in being true,
That honesty should start with me
In all I say, in all I do.
I'll form good habits in my youth,
To keep my word, to tell the truth,
To speak up in defending right
And keep my name and honor bright.
(Ruth Muir Gardner, "I Believe in Being Honest,"
Children's Songbook [Salt Lake City: The Church
of Jesus Christ of Latter-day Saints, 1989], p. 149.)

Who Is Your Hero?

The first step in being honest is to be honest with ourselves. This is also one of the first steps to happiness and to feelings of self-worth. We can never be at peace with God until we are honest with ourselves. The following story illustrates the importance of inner honesty.

A high school English teacher asked each student in her class to write down the name of his hero—the person he admired and looked up to the most. One of the boys in the class, whom we will call Phillip, wrote down the name of Jesus.

The teacher then asked each person to stand and reveal the name that he had written down. As the members of the class stood and announced their heroes, not one of them named a religious figure. As Phillip's turn approached, he felt embarrassed to say the name of Jesus, so he scratched it off and wrote down the name of a famous athlete. When Phillip's turn came, he lied about who his real hero was and told the class the name of the athlete.

There was a quiet, somewhat shy boy who sat three chairs behind Phillip. This boy had never said a single thing in class. When his turn came, he quietly stood and said that his hero was Jesus Christ. Phillip's heart was filled with admiration for this boy who had the honesty and courage to do what Phillip was afraid to do; but Phillip also felt a deep shame for not standing up for the Savior and telling the class the truth.

Even though Phillip admired the Savior, he had not

been active in the Church; but this experience changed that. Before class was over, Phillip decided that he would become active and would always stand up for the Savior. And this is exactly what he did.

Honesty begins inside a person. Because Phillip wasn't honest with himself, he wasn't honest with the class either. The class didn't know that he was lying, but he did; and this knowledge brought him much more pain and embarrassment than the class could ever have inflicted upon him. Your conscience can punish you much more than people can. On the other hand, when you are honest with yourself, you feel good inside, and the jeers or cruel comments of others are easier to handle.

We may fool others, but until we feel right within ourselves, we will never be truly happy. The following story not only depicts the sorrow that follows dishonesty but also demonstrates the feelings of peace and self-worth that come as we try to be honest.

A BYU student kept a wallet that she found in a phone booth because she needed the money it contained. At first she justified her act, but soon her conscience began to work on her. She had never been able to throw the wallet away, and nine years later she still had the wallet—and a lot of guilt and unhappiness.

One day as the former student looked through the wallet once again, she found a small, orange card that she had never noticed before. This piece of paper helped her trace the wallet's owner. She called the owner, a woman, and arranged to return the wallet. The owner of the wallet described their special meeting as follows:

> As though she had rehearsed this experience in her mind a hundred times, she reached out her steady hand, looked me squarely in the eye, and handed me the wallet. Her steady gaze reflected the radiance of a good and honest life.
>
> Then her eyes dropped as she whispered, "Will you

please forgive me? I want to be honest." Words would not come. I could only reach for her hand and nod affirmatively. From my office, I watched her walk away from my desk and out the front door. . . .

I went to the window to watch her with her shoulders square, head erect, and with a lilt in her step as she turned the corner out of sight. (Ardeth G. Kapp, "'Will You Please Forgive Me? I Want to Be Honest,'" *New Era*, July 1976, pp. 7–9.)

When the student first took the wallet, she sinned much more against herself than she did against the wallet's owner. When the girl finally made the decision to make things right, she blessed herself much more than she blessed anyone else. She walked away with her head erect and a lilt in her step because she was finally true to herself, to the other woman, and to God.

"We Either Die of Guilt or the Pinewood Paddle!"

A teacher tells the story about a test he gave in high school. His own brother was in the class, and when he corrected this brother's paper he noticed that his brother had written "I don't know this one" in response to one of the questions. A few papers later, the teacher corrected the test of his brother's friend, who also happened to sit next to this brother. On the same question the friend's paper said, "I don't know this one either." (From *Love Letter* [periodical], July 1988.)

Cheating is a major problem in our schools today. The young man described above was so used to copying his friend's papers that he even copied the incorrect answers written by his friend. Similarly, often the most serious sins in our lives are the sins that we are worrying about the least. This is because recognizing that we are doing something wrong and feeling bad about it are the first two steps of repentance. If we use this reasoning, it would appear that one of the most serious sins that many young people commit today is the sin of cheating. Some of these young people copy others' homework and cheat on tests and quizzes without giving it a second thought. In fact, many of them do not even consider these acts dishonest.

There are many ways to steal. One can steal money, physical possessions, time, grades, or credit for things he hasn't done. Cheating is not only stealing but also lying, for the cheater claims that the work he turns in is his own. A person needs only to listen to the promptings of the Spirit to know that all types of cheating are wrong. The following story shows how cheating can make the culprit feel if he is in tune with the Spirit.

Mrs. Frost was an eighth-grade teacher in a small town. She had a reputation as an excellent teacher who not only excelled in math and English but taught honesty, industry, charity, and many other virtues as well. Anyone who cheated in her class received several whacks from the pinewood paddle.

Mrs. Frost was Lanie and Sara's teacher in both Sunday School and public school. Just before the first test of the school year, Mrs. Frost took the paddle off the wall and said, "You are all on the honor system here. I will not allow you to mock your education by cheating. It is dishonest; it wastes your time and mine—and I'm too old to waste time. You may begin the test."

Lanie was really struggling with the test when her friend Sara shoved a piece of paper into her hand. As Lanie glanced at the paper, she realized that it contained the answers to the test. She quickly filled out her test, and she and Sara were the first ones finished.

The weekend after the test was the longest weekend of Lanie's life. On Friday night she had a horrible nightmare in which Mrs. Frost's face was on all of her stuffed animals. Lanie was afraid to go back to sleep for fear that she would have another nightmare, so she crept out of her window and went to Sara's house.

The first thing Sara said was, "I thought you were Mrs. Frost coming to take me away in the night." Sara was suffering as much as Lanie was.

On Saturday morning things got worse instead of better. Mrs. Frost called and asked both Lanie and Sara to help her with her Sunday School lesson. The scriptures she asked them to read were about honesty.

The two girls guiltily endured the lesson and were the first ones through the door when class was over. But they didn't get away without a warm thank-you from Mrs. Frost for their help with the lesson.

Both girls were very quiet on the way home until Sara said, "Did you see that? I think she had tears in her eyes when she thanked us. What are we gonna do?"

Lanie responded, "What choice do we have? We either die of guilt or the pinewood paddle."

Monday after school, the girls approached Mrs. Frost. They confessed that they had cheated, and asked for her forgiveness. In her Sunday School voice, Mrs. Frost said, "I'm so glad you came to me with this, girls. That took courage and shows a great deal of integrity. But you have made a sad mistake and must suffer the consequences. Not only will you lose the scores from these papers, but also the opportunity to learn from taking the test on your own. And, of course, the punishment for cheating in this classroom is a paddling."

In later years Lanie recalled that as Mrs. Frost reached for the paddle, "the horror stories of a generation of blistered bottoms flashed across" the girls' memories. Mrs. Frost said to them, "Now both of you close your eyes and keep them closed. What's about to happen is not a pretty sight."

Both girls were commanded to bend over the teacher's desk, and their legs started to shake as they awaited their punishment. Lanie was wondering which of them Mrs. Frost would spank first, when she heard a WHAP and realized the proceedings had begun with Sara. Lanie explains what happened next:

> Sara gave kind of a delayed little whimper which made me start to sniffle. Sara started to cry. I wanted to look, but dared not. I tried to relax for my swat.
>
> WHAP! Sara again, and that one sounded just wicked. Sara was sobbing by then. I joined in, out of sympathy or anxiety, I knew not.
>
> WHAP! Another to Sara. This was unmerciful. We both were wailing. I could take no more. "Please stop, Mrs. Frost! Sara, are you all right?"
>
> Simultaneously, we both looked up at each other across the big oak desk. Red faced and soggy, Sara answered, "What do you mean, am I all right? You're the one getting hit."
>
> As we stared at each other in confusion, WHAP! Mrs. Jayne Frost took one last swing and unloaded her padded desk chair of a decade's worth of dust. . . .
>
> . . . And then, speaking as she moved toward the door, Jayne Frost penned this line upon our memories forever: "I guess you might say this paddling was a lot like the knowledge you *could* have gained by taking the test on your own—neither one of you got it in the end."
>
> With that, she replaced the paddle upon the hook and left the room. (Lanie J. McMullin, "The Pinewood Paddle Massacre," *Ensign*, April 1991, pp. 65–66.)

Even though the girls cheated on the test, the fact that they felt guilty and tried to make things right shows that they were trying to live the gospel and were in tune with the Spirit. One function of the Spirit is to prod our conscience so that we feel guilty when we are doing something wrong. Those who cheat and don't feel guilty have hardened their hearts against the Spirit. Their growth toward eternal life will slow significantly unless they open their hearts to the Holy Ghost and respond to his guidance.

Remembering What Is Most Important

Several years ago Dr. Blake Smith, a non-Latter-day Saint, offered the following prayer before an "important" college game:

> Dear God: It is clear that Thou hast given us life with many different shades and colors. For this we are grateful. We humbly accept the fact that some things in our life are not very important.
>
> They are to be enjoyed but not taken too seriously. The occasion that brings us together is one of those happy interludes in life. Help us to accept it as such. In Thy presence we know that no issues of great importance are going to be settled here this afternoon. No souls are going to be lost or saved by the final figures on the scoreboard. No great cause is at stake. It is one of those pleasures which Thou hast meant for Thy children to enjoy.

Do not let us spoil it by forgetting that it is just a game to be enjoyed today, talked about tomorrow, and forgotten the day afterward. Keep us mindful of this, dear God, for we are human and easily lose our perspective and allow the things that are most important to become the victim of the things that are least important.

Because of the great emphasis that is placed on sports in our society, we can lose our perspective and think that winning is more important than honesty and sportsmanship. It is just as important to be honest on the court or the field as it is to be honest at other times in our lives. Winning a ball game or a championship means absolutely nothing when compared to receiving exaltation and eternal life. To win at sports through dishonesty is really to lose. Think about the relative importance of sports and honesty as you read the following story:

The very first Latter-day Saint that Mike ever met was Norman Taylor. Norman played on a soccer team with Mike, and all the players called him Norman the Mormon. His honesty and integrity made him unique among the young men on the team. Norman didn't smoke. He didn't drink beer, tea, or coffee. And he didn't swear or protest the referees' decisions.

One summer Mike's team reached the English youth cup final for the first time in the team's twenty-five-year history. In the championship game, with less than five minutes to go, the score was tied at a goal apiece. The other team mounted attack after attack. Following a corner kick, the ball bounced off a couple of players and appeared to hit Norman's hand. The other team immediately appealed for a penalty kick because of the apparent violation, and Mike's team denied their appeal.

Neither the referee nor the linesman had seen the incident. Knowing Norman's beliefs, the referee asked him if he had touched the ball with his hand. Norman quietly answered, "Yes, I did." The referee awarded the other team a penalty kick, which was then converted. Moments later the game was over—Mike's team had lost 2–1.

As the team filed dejectedly into their dressing room, not one player said an unkind word or made a scene. Norman sat with his face in his hands, quietly weeping at their loss.

Mike recalls that he and the team learned a great lesson that day. Mike later joined the Church and moved to Utah.

Norman is a young man who is well along the path of celestial growth. He has made commitments of honesty and integrity that seem to be able to withstand any trial. As a result Norman has earned the respect of players, of officials, of spectators—and of God. Many people have used his honesty and courage as an example since the day of that soccer game. Although some may ridicule those who do right, most people respect and admire the person who will stand up for his convictions, no matter the consequence.

As you consider the honesty of Norman, you might ask yourself two good questions: If I had been in Norman's situation, would I have told the truth? Do I practice honesty in the sports in which I participate?

Ideas to Remember

1. Honesty comes from within. A truly honest person will be honest under all circumstances.

2. Feelings of peace and self-worth come to us when we are honest and true to ourselves. On the other hand, when we are dishonest, we hurt ourselves much more than we hurt others.

3. Cheating involves both stealing and lying and is a serious form of dishonesty.

4. Feeling guilty when we have done something wrong is a blessing, for it helps us to repent and make things right.

5. It is easy to lose one's perspective and begin to think that winning a ball game or a championship is more important than being fair and honest and displaying good sportsmanship.

6. Our quest for celestial life is one not just of doing but of becoming, and one of the things we must become is totally honest—honest with ourselves, with others, and with God.

8

No Greater Joy

Have I done any good in the world today?
Have I helped anyone in need?
Have I cheered up the sad and made someone feel glad?
If not, I have failed indeed.
(Will L. Thompson, "Have I Done Any Good?"
Hymns, no. 223.)

A Feeling to Work For

As the alarm went off, Roy turned over and pushed the snooze button to buy himself more time. It was Sunday and there wasn't much reason to get out of bed. Lately every Sunday had been a pretty ho-hum day. Roy taught the adult Gospel Doctrine class in his ward, and this year he was teaching the New Testament course for the fourth time. Preparation for class had been a little tough the first two times, but now Roy's lessons were ready and he seldom bothered to review them.

Roy crossed his hands behind his head and thought about that day's lesson. It wasn't anything to get excited about. He knew the story by heart—but then, so did everyone else in the class. The parable of the Good Samaritan was one that they had all learned in Primary years ago. Roy sighed as he thought of this ho-hum lesson to match his ho-hum day. *Oh well,* he thought, *I'll get through this one and so will the rest of the class.*

As Roy's class ended later that morning, he felt that he had covered all of the essential points of the parable, and as usual he had committed the class to apply what they had learned.

The next day Roy's work schedule was full. He and several other managers had a one o'clock meeting with the boss. Roy and his boss were both sticklers for punctuality, so Roy had planned his day accordingly. He didn't want to be in the same boat with the men who had arrived late to other meetings and were forced to endure the heckling that followed.

Roy made several morning calls on customers, then stopped to get a quick bite to eat before going to the meeting. The restaurant's quick service fit right into his schedule, and he left the table with fifteen minutes to spare. But the first step out the door, Roy was hit square in the face with a decision.

Two middle-aged ladies were standing beside their car, looking at a flat rear tire. It was obvious that they didn't have a clue how to change it.

Roy's first thought was Christian enough. He immediately turned to help them, but as he turned he simultaneously remembered the meeting and knew that he couldn't help the ladies and get to the meeting on time. With a pang of guilt, he turned the other way, thinking that someone else would surely stop.

Heading for his car, Roy kept glancing back at the ladies to make sure they would be assisted. He watched from his car with disgust as two grown men walked past the women without even hesitating. Then another man walked by, looking right at them but not stopping. When two teenage boys walked by without assisting the stranded pair, Roy reached for his car door handle, thinking, *What's the matter with people today?* Then it hit him—a statement he'd made the day before: "Let's all try to be like the Good Samaritan and help someone truly in need." He would just have to be late for his meeting.

Roy walked over to the women and asked them if he could help. The owner of the car replied with a grateful "Yes, please." She explained that she and her friend had a meeting to get to, and they had no idea how to change a tire.

Roy quickly took off the flat tire and replaced it with the spare. This job would not have been a problem had he been dressed in his old work clothes, but it took a little longer with the maneuvers he had to perform to keep the dirt and grease limited to his hands.

A sincere thank-you was received, and Roy pushed the pedal as far as he dared in his rush to the meeting. When he arrived he stepped into a restroom to wash his hands before facing the taunting looks and comments of his peers.

As Roy washed his hands he glanced in the mirror, and then it hit him. He took a long look, and he liked what he saw. It wasn't his face or his hair or anything physical. It was a feeling inside—a feeling that radiated out through his eyes. Nothing the other managers could say to him could take this feeling away. It was something that was higher and more powerful than any cutting remarks they could throw at him. He felt that he had walked for one morning in the shoes of the Good Samaritan. And the resulting feeling was worth every minute he had spent in service.

Service that brings the good feeling that Roy experienced is not usually convenient or easy to give. Sometimes we may even be asked to serve someone we do not like. It takes effort to recognize those who need our service.

President Spencer W. Kimball was always looking for opportunities to serve. These opportunities often presented themselves at inconvenient times. Elder H. Burke Peterson related one such experience:

> A few years ago I had been assigned with other General Authorities to attend a series of area conferences in New Zealand and Australia. Initially, the leader of our group was to have been President Spencer W. Kimball. However, because of the need for some emergency surgery, he could not travel with us, so President N. Eldon Tanner led the group in his place.
>
> Each day during the trip President Tanner telephoned President Kimball in his hospital room to get a report on his condition and to give a brief report of the conferences in which we were participating. After the daily call to Salt

Lake City, President Tanner would always give us a report on the President's condition. We were anxious and appreciated these brief messages.

Once, after we had been out for five or six days, President Tanner made his usual call to the hospital in Salt Lake City. However, this day he had no report for us. When we asked if he had talked to the President, he told us he had tried, but President Kimball wasn't in his room. "Where was he?" we asked. "They weren't sure; they couldn't find him," President Tanner said. "They thought he might have gone down to the next floor of the hospital to visit the sick." ("Selflessness: A Pattern for Happiness," *Ensign*, May 1985, p. 65.)

The Mess

Elder Williams was excited. President Kendall, his mission president, had called him in to assign him to a new area and a new companion. Elder Williams had liked his last area but had become discouraged with his companion's lack of desire to work. He wanted a fresh start and was excited about the possibilities of this new situation.

President Kendall talked with Elder Williams about his mission and his goals. The young missionary could feel his excitement building as President Kendall identified his new area and said that his new companion would be Elder Sorenson. Elder Williams didn't know Elder Sorenson, but he had heard about him. He knew that Elder Sorenson was a real go-getter. He worked hard and was often in the top baptizing area.

President Kendall told Elder Williams that his new companion had only four months left to serve and that this area would be Elder Sorenson's last. The president also said it was very likely that Elder Williams would be his last companion. Elder Williams knew he could look forward to four good months of missionary work.

Elder Williams and Elder Sorenson had a blissful first week. Their personalities were so much alike, and the missionary work took off immediately. There was just one problem—Elder Sorenson's housekeeping skills were basically nonexistent. To put it bluntly, he lived like a pig.

At first it didn't seem like that big a deal; Elder Williams decided that he would just have to put up with this one flaw and save his energy for missionary work. But this "one flaw" gnawed at Elder Williams. His excitement level stayed up while he and his companion were out doing missionary work. But his enthusiasm always faded when they entered their messy apartment and waded through the clothing that was scattered about.

After three weeks Elder Williams had reached his limit. He decided that a heart-to-heart talk about cleanliness couldn't hurt, but Elder Sorenson laughed and said that the mess wasn't a big deal. When Elder Williams insisted that it *was* a big deal to him, Elder Sorenson shrugged and said that he had always lived this way and that it was too late for him to change. He told Elder Williams that he would just have to live with the mess.

Elder Williams tried for three more weeks to put up with the mess, but his intolerance and disgust grew as the mess grew. He knew that it was futile to talk to Elder Sorenson, so he went to Elder Albert, the district leader, and told him that he wanted to be transferred.

Elder Albert responded that he needed to learn to love his companion for his good qualities. They talked about what those good qualities were and how they outweighed the mess in the apartment. But Elder Williams insisted that he had already tried that kind of positive thinking. What he needed was a change, and he pleaded with Elder Albert to grant his request. Elder Albert still insisted that he needed to learn to love Elder Sorenson—then he would be able to overlook the mess. Elder Williams replied that he didn't think he could ever love Elder Sorenson as long as he was so messy.

It was at this point that Elder Albert wisely proposed an experiment. Elder Albert asked him to shine Elder Sorenson's shoes and iron his shirt while Elder Sorenson was in the shower. He also instructed him not to say anything about it to Elder Sorenson. Elder Williams consented to do these things but wondered how this was going to solve the problem.

The next morning when Elder Sorenson went in the bathroom, Elder Williams got the shoes out and buffed them to what he thought was a beautiful shine. He then meticulously ironed the shirt and returned it to its hanger. He thought to himself that it would be exciting to see the look on Elder Sorenson's face when he discovered the shoes and the shirt.

Elder Sorenson came out of the bathroom, took his shirt from the closet, and started ironing it. Then, as he had done every other morning, Elder Sorenson took his shoes out and started shining them. Elder Williams was disgusted. He had wasted his good time doing something that wasn't even appreciated.

That morning Elder Albert called the two elders and asked if he could drop by before they went out proselyting. Elder Williams could hardly wait to let him know what had happened. When Elder Albert arrived, Elder Williams pulled him aside and told him the story. Elder Albert's reaction surprised him. The district leader very calmly said, "Do it again tomorrow, and keep doing it until we see each other again." Elder Williams reluctantly agreed.

The next morning he carefully ironed the shirt and shined the shoes—with the same results. This went on for several days. Each day saw Elder Williams getting madder and madder, until one morning something very interesting happened. As he waited for Elder Sorenson to come out of the bathroom, a wonderful feeling came over him. Elder Williams felt an all-consuming love for his companion. Suddenly all he could think about was the good that Elder Sorenson had done for him. His anxiety over the mess in the apartment seemed to be swept from his mind.

Elder Williams realized immediately that this great feeling was a gift from Heavenly Father. He also realized that what mattered most was the work that he was doing as a missionary, and this work would never go forth until there was a true feeling of love between him and his companion. Elder Sorenson's mess was not important enough to stop the Lord's work.

With these thoughts in mind, he watched Elder Sorenson come out of the bathroom, get his shirt out of the closet, and look at it closely on both sides. With a questioning look on his face, he turned to Elder Williams and asked, "Did you iron my shirt?" Elder Williams just smiled when Elder Sorenson took out his already-polished shoes and started to shine them.

Elder Williams learned a great lesson that day. He discovered that Heavenly Father's power is always with those who render selfless service to his children. It is through that power that our problems can be solved. President Kimball taught: "It is by serving that we learn how to serve. When we are engaged in the service of our fellowmen, not only do our deeds assist them, but we put our own problems in a fresher perspective. When we concern ourselves more with others, there is less time to be concerned with ourselves. In the midst of the miracle of serving, there is the promise of Jesus, that by losing ourselves, we find ourselves." ("Small Acts of Service," *Ensign*, December 1974, p. 2.)

The Wrong Exit

It was one o'clock in the afternoon, and Jared was starving. His early breakfast had worn off by midmorning, but he had been too busy at the office to stop working. As he drove down the freeway, he looked for a place to grab a quick bite to eat. A glance at the signs indicated that one of his favorite fast-food places was just off the next exit. He took the exit and drove into the parking lot.

Deciding that he needed to take a real break for lunch, he opted to eat inside instead of using the drive-through window. He walked into the restaurant and got in line behind several other people. As he waited, he sensed that something was wrong. He had a strange feeling that he was being watched. As he surveyed the restaurant, it became apparent to him why he was feeling uncomfortable. He had obviously taken the wrong exit. His skin was several shades lighter than that of anyone else in the restaurant. All the workers at the counter, all the cooks, and all the other customers were black.

As he moved closer to the counter, he became more and more uncomfortable. He imagined what was going through the minds of the customers and employees: *What is this white man doing? Doesn't he know he isn't suppose to be in here?*

With one person between him and the counter, he reached into his pocket to get some change. He wanted to have his money ready so that he could place his order and pay for it quickly. He would further cut down the time by making his order "to go."

Just then a man behind him tapped him on the shoulder. Jared jumped, then turned around quickly to see what was the matter. A dark, friendly face said, "Excuse me, you dropped this." Jared looked down to see a hundred-dollar bill in the man's hand. With a quiet "Thank you," he took back the money. It must have fallen out of his pocket as he fished for change.

By this time Jared had reached the counter. Still flustered by the kindness of the man behind him, he stumbled through his order. The clerk was pleasant and helpful. She seemed oblivious to his skin color. Jared thanked her as he received his food and then turned around quickly to head for the door.

Not two steps later, a woman bumped into Jared, spilling his drink all over the floor. Before he could react, she was apologizing for spilling the drink. Another woman was already cleaning up the mess. As she wiped up the drink, Jared felt a warm, peaceful feeling spread from his head to his toes. He knew why these people were being so good to him in spite of his white skin. They knew what true service was. They understood that true service doesn't see the color of a person's skin or the way he is dressed or how old he is. True service is given without prejudice.

Jared now knew that what he had thought to be the wrong exit was really the right exit. In fact, it was probably the best exit he had ever taken in his life.

Elder Hans B. Ringger echoed the lesson that Jared learned, when he stated: "We need to look around us, and if we cannot see poverty, illness, and despair in our own neighborhood or ward, then we have to look harder. And remember, we cannot be afraid to go beyond our own social and cultural circles. We have to rid ourselves of religious, racial, or social prejudices and expand the boundaries of our service. Service should never discriminate and is hardly ever easy." ("'Choose You This Day,'" *Ensign,* May 1990, p. 26.)

The kind of service that really carries the power to make one happy is unconditional service. This means that one serves for the sake of service. There are no strings attached.

There are two powerful types of unconditional service. The first is serving those we dislike. These are often the people who need our service the most, but they are also the people it takes the greatest effort to serve. Many times, the harder it is to serve someone, the greater will be the joy and happiness experienced by the giver and the receiver.

The second powerful form of unconditional service is anonymous service. Anonymous service helps us keep our motives pure. If we know that no one is going to praise our service with a "Thank you" or a "Good job," then we are likely serving with a higher purpose. The Savior described anonymous service this way: "When thou doest alms let not thy left hand know what thy right hand doeth; that thine alms may be in secret; and thy Father who seeth in secret, himself shall reward thee openly" (3 Nephi 13:3–4).

The game of volleyball teaches a great principle with regard to true service. You can only score in volleyball when you serve. So it is with the game of life—the real scores in life are made when we render pure service.

Ideas to Remember

1. We learn to love those whom we serve. The best way to increase our love for someone is to serve him or her.

2. Heavenly Father knows who needs our service the most. Ask him every day in your prayers to lead you to those in need. Then watch throughout the day for opportunities to serve those who need you.

3. Everyone can do something. You don't have to do something great or give some big gift. Every little act of service makes a difference.

4. Try to serve anonymously when you can. When we offer service without seeking recognition, we are more likely to serve for the right reasons. We serve because we truly want to, and not because others are watching us or because we expect something in return.

9

Music Is the Language of the Soul

The Lord has said a heartfelt song
By righteous ones is prayer;
A hymn unites us and invites
The Spirit to be there
(Penelope Moody Allen, "With Songs
of Praise," *Hymns,* no. 71).

"I Think She's Dying"

LDS musician Lex de Azevedo gave this vivid description of the power of music: "Music has been called the universal language. It is a language more powerful than words, for it is the language of emotion. Words communicate ideas; music communicates feelings. While words get stuck in the thinking part of our brains, music sails through to reach the innermost corners of our emotional being. And it is our emotions and feelings which really govern our lives and our actions. This is precisely why music is such a wonderful, dangerous, exhilarating, exciting power." (*Pop Music and Morality* [North Hollywood, Calif.: Embryo Books, 1982], p. 37.)

All through history, people have used music to draw closer to God and receive strength, comfort, and blessings from him. The Savior sang a hymn just before he suffered for our sins in the Garden of Gethsemane. Joseph Smith received great comfort and strength from a hymn shortly before he was killed by a mob. The pioneers sang many hymns as they made their difficult way across the American plains. A certain kind of music can put us in contact with God through his Spirit.

Dave and Deborah Smoot had an experience with music that actually led to the saving of a young woman's life. The Smoot family had planned a vacation, but the day of departure had been a long and trying one. Deborah had been left with all of the packing, and Dave, a surgeon in training, was detained at the hospital. Before they even got out of the city, the children were restless and bored and the parents were snapping at each other.

Deborah placed a tape of Primary songs into the car cassette player and sat back to endure her anger in silence. Because of music's great power to reach the heart and feelings, the whole family was soon singing the chorus of "The Still Small Voice": "Listen, listen. The Holy Ghost will whisper. Listen, listen to the still small voice." As the song ended, Dave said that they needed to turn around. Suddenly the whole family felt the same need to go back.

It was not long before they approached a man standing beside a parked truck. The man flagged them down and told them that a girl riding a motorcycle had been involved in an accident. The man then added, "I think she's dying." As they looked down the hill, they could see a body and a mangled motorcycle lying about fifty yards away. While Dave grabbed his emergency kit and headed for the injured girl, his wife and children knelt in prayer.

The young woman was unconscious and was not breathing, but because of some equipment Dave had recently purchased at a hospital sale, and with the help of his CPR skills, Dave was able to breathe for the girl, and probably saved her life. Dave rode with the girl in the ambulance, started an IV for her, and talked on the ambulance radio with the people at the hospital so they would be ready when the ambulance arrived.

As Deborah drove behind the ambulance, her mind was racing: "What if we hadn't had the first-aid kit? What if Dave hadn't gone to the hospital sale? What if he hadn't been trained in CPR? And most of all, what if we had continued to argue instead of sing? Would we have then heard the 'still small voice'? Would we have recognized it?" (See Deborah Smoot, "'Listen, Listen,'" *Ensign*, February 1990, p. 68–69.)

One of the most important things we can ever do in this life is learn to recognize and respond to the promptings of the Holy Ghost. Few things have greater power to bring the Spirit or drive it away than does music. At a critical time, music replaced an atmosphere of anger and contention with one of peace and unity and a family was able to receive the promptings of the Spirit. Music can do the same for us—it can help to create an atmosphere where the Spirit can dwell. Music can help us sort through the conflicts in our lives and receive the peace and guidance that we desire.

"Our Music Is Calculated to Drive Them to Sex!"

If we consider the great power music has to touch and change our inner selves, and if we then think about how many thousands of hours we listen to music, it doesn't take long to realize how influential music really is in our lives. It seems wise to make the decision that we will carefully choose the type of music we are going to invite into our hearts and minds.

Sometimes we underestimate the good or the bad that music is doing to our souls. This problem was discussed by Lex de Azevedo:

> Whether we like it or not, we are at war! We are fighting a life-and-death battle for the human soul, and our enemies are Lucifer and his hosts. . . . The battlefield is the birthplace of all human action—the mind.

Music is one of the adversary's deadliest weapons. Using it he creates sugar-coated poison that can slowly destroy all our brightest dreams and leave us spiritually dead. The irony is that we take this deadly thing voluntarily into our homes, schools, and churches. Some surround themselves with it twenty-four hours a day. We share it with our loved ones. We pay millions of dollars a year for the privilege of exposing ourselves to it. Like foolish Trojans, we open the gates of our strongholds and let the enemy in. . . .

. . . We should understand that it is the deadliest war of all. In a physical war, we at least know when we've been wounded, maimed, or killed. But in spiritual battles, Satan's bullets come with their own novocaine. Each time we are hit we feel less pain. The more hits we take the more desensitized we become. With our spiritual life oozing out of us, we continue to proclaim, "But it doesn't really affect me!" (*Pop Music and Morality*, pp. 113, 114–15.)

When someone attacks the music we like, we usually feel that they are attacking us, and we vigorously step forward to defend our music. Perhaps this is because the music we listen to has become part of our personal feelings and emotions. Some people try to place music into categories, such as hard rock, soft rock, country and western, rap, or religious. They then say that one of these types of music is good or that one of them is bad. There are good and bad songs in every category of music, so this effort to make black-and-white distinctions just doesn't work.

Since our goal is to grow spiritually and become more like our Father in Heaven, it is up to us to decide which songs and which performers lead us closer to him and which ones take us further away. As we seriously decide to choose music that is good for us and avoid music that destroys us spiritually, we can seek the help of the Holy Ghost. Because of the importance of music, he will guide us in this selection process.

It is important to realize that much of the harmful music that is available today has been deliberately made to achieve certain effects. There are many writers and performers who are anti-God and anti-good. They actively promote such things as immorality, violence, homosexuality, Satan-worship, rebellion, and the destruction of society and the family. These people have specific immoral messages that they are trying to promote with their music.

The following story is about a popular performer whose standards are very different from those established by the Lord. The authors are sharing this story because it is vital that you realize that many performers are trying to destroy your faith and your values through their music.

One of the General Authorities, Elder Gene R. Cook, was flying back from Mexico to the United States. He wanted to share the gospel with the man sitting next to him on the plane, so he offered a silent prayer that the Lord would help him know what to say. Elder Cook then introduced himself, said that he was a member of The Church of Jesus Christ of Latter-day Saints, and asked the man what his name was. The man answered, "My name is Mick Jagger."

Not realizing that he was the famous Mick Jagger, Elder Cook said, "Well, I'm glad to meet you, Mick."

The man growled, "I said, my name is *Mick Jagger*."

When Elder Cook responded, "I heard you, Mick," the man opened up a magazine and pointed to a photo of himself. Finally Elder Cook realized whom he was talking to.

Before sharing this story with a group of young people, Elder Cook made it very clear that he was not going to speak evil of Mr. Jagger, but that he was going to speak against the things Mick Jagger represented, for they were sponsored by the devil.

The two men chatted for a few minutes, and then Elder Cook said, "You know, Mick—I have a question that I would like you to answer for me."

Elder Cook then told the singer of the opportunity he had as a General Authority to talk with young people all over the world. He explained that some of these young people had told him that Mick Jagger's kind of music—the kind that Jagger and others like him played—had no effect on them. They claimed that it was OK to listen to because it didn't affect them adversely in any way. Elder Cook said that other young people had told him that Jagger's type of music was harmful to them, that it affected them in a very real way—for evil. Elder Cook then said, "You've been in this business for a very long time, Mick. I would like to know your opinion. What do you think is the impact of your music on the young people?"

He shocked Elder Cook when he replied, "Our music is calculated to drive the kids to sex." He quickly added, "It's not my fault what they do—that's up to them. I'm just making a lot of money."

Jagger proudly shared the fact that he had fathered three children out of wedlock. He went on to explain that this was a great day for performers like himself, because with music videos, entertainers could portray sex on the screen, as well as have it written into the lyrics. Because of the extra dimension provided by videos, Jagger said, he and others like him were making a much greater impact on young people, besides making a lot more money.

As the two men talked over the next few hours, they found that they disagreed on every important issue. Jagger didn't believe there was a God or a judgment day, and felt that a person could do whatever he wanted or take whatever he wanted without suffering any consequences. He was grateful that the family was being destroyed and felt that young people ought to be able to do anything they wanted to do, in spite of their parents' wishes.

Toward the end of their discussion, Jagger made the mistake of saying, "Your Book of Mormon is a lie, and any man who believes it is a liar." He said this loud enough that the people sitting around them could hear it.

Elder Cook responded by saying, "Well, Mick, you're fortunate today—mighty fortunate." When Jagger asked why, Elder Cook replied, "Because you are sitting next to a servant of the Lord, who plans on correcting what you just said."

When the singer asked what he meant, Elder Cook said, "You are lucky that I just happen to have a Book of Mormon right here in my briefcase." Elder Cook then pulled out his own copy of the Book of Mormon, handed it to Jagger, and said, "Mick, this book has changed my life. I love the Book of Mormon. I've read it many times, and it is the greatest book—in my mind—on the face of the earth. In my view it has made me a better man. You say it's a lie. I must have missed that part—show me."

There was total silence. When Jagger didn't say anything, Elder Cook continued, "Maybe you were offended by the part where Lehi told his sons to be honest men and taught them to rely upon the Lord and have faith in God. Maybe you were offended when Alma told his boy Corianton that he had broken the law of chastity and told him what he needed to do to correct it. Maybe it was the part when Christ came that really bothered you—when he said that you are to love thy wife with all thy heart and not commit adultery."

Elder Cook finally said, "If you can't show me a chapter, then show me a page or even one paragraph."

Once again there was dead silence, and after asking Jagger to show him a line or even a word that was a lie, Elder Cook bore a strong spiritual witness of the Book of Mormon and said: "My friend, the lie is not in the Book of Mormon—the lie is in you." (13 *Lines of Defense—Living the Law of Chastity* [Salt Lake City: Deseret Book Company, 1991], audiocassette, side 3.)

As you think about this conversation, which man do you want to listen to and follow? One man teaches that self-control and moral cleanliness bring happiness. The other boasts that his music is designed to lead people to immorality and claims that there are no rules that matter anyway. Which man cares about you and your future happiness?

Because there really is music that invites the Spirit of the Lord and music that invites the devil, it is critically important to choose carefully what we listen to. If we listen to Satan's music, it will negatively affect our thoughts and emotions, and we will eventually behave the way Satan wants us to. On the other hand, God's music leads to spiritual thoughts, which then lead to righteous actions. The influences with which you surround yourself will slowly but surely determine the kind of person you become.

They Choked on Lyrics That Called the Lord a Joke

In 1975 a professional show called *Music, America!* was organized. The new building that housed the show seated eighteen hundred people, and a twenty-one-piece orchestra was carefully selected to accompany the on-stage performers. Of the fourteen hundred young people who auditioned, eighteen singer-dancers were hired. Tailors measured each of them for custom-fit costumes—even their fingers and thumbs were measured for individualized gloves. The rehearsals were rigorous, but the future opportunities for the young performers were limitless.

Three exhilarating weeks of rehearsal had rushed by when things suddenly grew dark for the four Latter-day Saint performers in the show. When they received their script for the rock-and-roll segment, it was filled with sac-

rilegious words referring to the Savior. As the group prac-
ticed that afternoon, the voices of the four Latter-day
Saints faltered. The two returned missionaries and two
young women, as the author who later wrote of their
experience put it, "choked on lyrics that called the Lord a
joke, a fraud."

During that rehearsal each of the four LDS performers
made a private decision to leave the show. None of them
felt that they could sing words that were offensive to
themselves and to God.

When the four talked to the director, he asked them to
consider what they were giving up and talk with him
again in the morning. They realized that they were not
indispensable, for there were 1396 other young people
who would be eager and willing to replace them.

The four spent many hours that night discussing their
choices, but they concluded that they really had no
options. They recommitted themselves to leave the show
"rather than make a mockery of their Savior."

After two vigorous hours of rehearsal the next morning, the director approached Steve, one of the LDS performers, and asked him if all four of them still felt the
same way. When Steve quietly answered that they still
didn't feel that they could perform the offensive musical
number, the director paused for a moment and said,
"Well, I've given it a lot of thought since we talked. I don't
want to scratch the piece. I'm not trying to make some
kind of a statement, but I need it to round out the history
of rock in America. How would this work—would you
have any objections to going offstage for this bit? I think
I've figured out a way to work around you, make it a
smaller group. How would you feel about that?"

Steve answered, "We don't have the right to dictate
what you put in your show. It's just that we can't take part
in anything so foreign to our religious beliefs. If we are
completely out of that section, that's all we have a right to
ask."

Opening night arrived and the building was packed. Author Kris Mackay described what happened next:

> As the fast-paced show continued, it was evident that it was a hit. The atmosphere was wholesome and witty, typical of all that is good in America. There had been wild applause and spontaneous standing ovations throughout.
>
> Then, without warning, the raucous beat of *Jesus Christ, Super Star* pulsed through the air. Fourteen performers in fringed costumes gyrated through four minutes of music and dance as out of place in that setting as if someone had stomped on the American flag. An almost inaudible gasp swept through the audience. At the end of the number four shadowy figures slipped back through the wings, unobtrusively joining in the smash finale.
>
> The show was over. Eighteen hundred people leaped to their feet. The applause was deafening.
>
> As the audience filed out, the cast gathered behind closed curtains to review the performance. The director complimented them on a job well done, mentioned several places in need of a bit of smoothing out, and, almost as an afterthought, said, "Oh, yes. It ran a little long. We need to cut something. Let's skip over 'Super Star' starting with the next show." (See *No Greater Love* [Salt Lake City: Deseret Book Company, 1982] pp. 10–14.)

Steve and his friends had a great love for music, but they had an even greater love for the Savior. That is why they were willing to drop out of the show and sacrifice future musical opportunities that might come their way. Singing a song that mocks the Savior, night after night, would have driven the Spirit out of their lives. And listening to inappropriate music will have the same effect on us.

Our choice of music may not determine whether or not we are in a hit show, but it is certain that it will affect whether or not we receive inspiration and guidance from the Holy Ghost. It may take courage to leave a dance or a concert or a party where inappropriate music is being played. Friends who do not understand our values and goals may put pressure on us to stay. But with the Lord's help, we can develop the courage to purge evil music from our lives and replace it with music that moves us to good works and increases our reverence for things of the Spirit.

A Heavenly Choir

Have you ever considered how important music is to God? Music seems to be just as important in heaven as it is here on earth. When the heavens were opened to the prophet Lehi, he saw that the Lord was surrounded with numberless concourses of angels who were singing and praising their God (see 1 Nephi 1:8). Just before his death, King Benjamin was looking forward to joining "the choirs above in singing the praises of a just God" (Mosiah 2:28).

What a blessing it would be to hear the angels sing. What sweet music must come from the mouths of these pure beings as they sing praises of love and appreciation to our Heavenly Parents. In the following story, one couple who had this special opportunity share their experience with us.

Don and his wife served as custodians at their local chapel. During the winter they had to get a fire going in the old chapel stove by five o'clock on Sunday mornings in order for the building to be warm enough for the nine o'clock priesthood meeting.

On one such morning, long before the sun came up,

they pulled on their warm clothes and climbed into their car. Even though the morning was cold, it was so bright and beautiful that they didn't even bother to turn the car headlights on. As they drove slowly through the magnificent winter panorama, they could hear the ice crystals crunching under the wheels of the car.

They coasted up to the front of the chapel and stopped the car. When they turned the key off, they could hear singing coming from the church. A choir was singing a hymn that both Don and his wife were familiar with. They listened to the music for awhile and commented on how beautiful it was. All of a sudden his wife said, "Hey, there's not supposed to be anybody in there."

They both got out of the car and walked quietly toward the chapel. As they walked they could still hear the singing. When they reached the front door, Don's wife told him to wait a few minutes before entering, until she could run around to the back door.

After waiting for her to reach the other door, Don got out his keys and proceeded to unlock the front door. As soon as he touched the door, the music stopped. When he entered the chapel and turned the lights on, he found that the chapel was empty. About this time his wife came in from the back, having seen no one leave.

Don shared this experience with his bishop and others and said that he never cleaned the building again without feeling that his job was a special one. He was convinced that the chapel was in use much more than the ward members realized. He was so grateful that the Lord had allowed him to listen through the veil and hear the angels sing.

After hearing this story, there have been many times when we, the authors, have passed our own ward chapels and wondered if they were being used by angels. We have wondered as we have sung in our meetings if angels might be singing with us.

The authors came to appreciate the great power of Church hymns when we toured the land of Israel. We soon learned that the singing of hymns brought the Spirit of the Lord. For example, when we visited the traditional site of Jesus' birth, we had a somewhat empty feeling. Then someone started singing "Away in a Manger," and we all joined in. Within seconds the Spirit entered our hearts, and we felt a great love and appreciation for Jesus. Tears came to our eyes as we felt the Spirit testify of the birth of the Savior. We had similar experiences at other sites as we poured out our hearts to God through music.

In July 1830 the Lord commanded Emma Smith to gather a collection of sacred hymns for the Saints (see D&C 25). She was promised that the Lord would help her choose hymns that were pleasing to him. The Lord explained how he feels when we sincerely sing music that has been written to teach, uplift, and inspire: "For my soul delighteth in the song of the heart; yea, the song of the righteous is a prayer unto me, and it shall be answered with a blessing upon their heads" (D&C 25:12).

When we participate in our church meetings by singing the hymns, our heartfelt singing is counted as a prayer unto God and he blesses us for it. Among the immediate blessings that come are the feeling of unity with the others who are singing and the feelings of peace and reverence as we receive the Spirit and commune with God.

It is significant that the sacrament meeting prayers—the invocation, benediction, and sacrament prayers—are preceded by hymns. Singing invites the Spirit into our hearts so that we are ready to speak with our Heavenly Father and make covenants with him.

As we sing the hymns and pay attention to the words, we will receive peace and strength that will bring new dimensions to our worship. As we commit the hymns to memory, we can carry them with us, and they will serve as a source of comfort and encouragement wherever we go.

Ideas to Remember

1. Music can be more powerful than words because it has the power to reach our innermost feelings.
2. A certain kind of music can put us in contact with God through his Spirit. Few things have greater power to invite or repel the Spirit than does music.
3. Music is one of Satan's deadliest weapons, yet with their spiritual life oozing out of them, some people continue to proclaim, "But it doesn't really affect me!"
4. The Lord will help us decide which music is good for us and which music will destroy us spiritually.
5. Some writers and performers are anti-God and anti-good. They deliberately create music that undermines our beliefs and destroys our souls.
6. Because there really is music of the Lord and music of the devil, it is critically important to carefully choose what we listen to.
7. With the Lord's help, we can develop the courage to purge evil music from our lives and replace it with music that moves us to good works and increases our reverence for things of the Spirit.
8. Singing the Church hymns brings the Spirit of the Lord.
9. The Lord delights in the song of the heart, and the song of the righteous is a prayer unto him.
10. Singing the hymns at our church meetings is an important part of our worship. It brings feelings of peace and reverence as we receive the Spirit and commune with our Father in Heaven.

10

Living the Word of Wisdom

Our Father in Heaven has promised
Sound wisdom, knowledge, and health
If obedient to his word of wisdom
These treasures will be your wealth
(Clara W. McMaster, "His Promise," *Sing with Me: Songs for Children* [Salt Lake City: Deseret Book Company, 1969], B-34).

"Never"

Life had been good to Larry. He had been blessed with good parents, who had fully supported him in all of his endeavors. After graduating from high school, he went to college; there he met and fell in love with Janice. Shortly after Larry graduated from college, he and Janice were married in a beautiful garden ceremony.

Larry's success and happiness continued. He landed a good job, and over the next few years his possessions grew and so did his family. At their tenth wedding anniversary, Larry knew there was no one with a richer life than he. He counted his wife and his four children as his greatest joys.

On the first weekend after his anniversary, Larry was fishing with a longtime friend. They talked about their lives and their happiness. As Larry expressed how much his family meant to him, his friend asked a pointed question: "Larry, would you ever consider giving up your family for something else?" Larry's response was an emphatic "Never!" By the tone of his voice and by the conviction with which he stated his answer, his friend knew that Larry really meant what he said. The sad truth is that Larry did give up his family.

Larry loved to fish and hunt. While he was on these fishing and hunting trips, he began to drink a few beers. Over a period of time, those few beers turned into many. It wasn't long before Larry started drinking at home. Soon those drinks multiplied until his home drinking became an everyday routine. Each day as he arrived home from work, he would begin drinking. Eventually, most of his evenings were spent in a drunken stupor in front of the television. Soon he was drinking at work. That drinking escalated until he was asked to resign his position.

As the days went on and Larry's drinking continued to destroy more pieces of their lives, Larry and Janice drifted further and further apart. Janice desperately wanted to save their marriage. She approached him time and again about his alcoholism, trying to offer the love and support she knew he would need in order to change, but her concern was thrown back at her with loud verbal abuse. The children no longer wanted to be around their dad and were embarrassed to bring their friends home.

It was a sad day indeed when Janice told Larry to leave. Her beautiful marriage was gone, and the man she had known and loved had been destroyed by alcohol. Larry left home, never to return. He lived the rest of his life from one drink to the next. Jobless—and often homeless—he lived a meager existence with very little contact with Janice and the children. His life finally came to a premature end as a result of his heavy drinking.

Larry's story is a sad one. Tragically, this story doesn't belong just to Larry but has been repeated again and again throughout the history of man. The most tragic word of Larry's story is the word *never*. Larry made the statement that he would never give up his family. Others have said that they would never take the life of another human being. Some insist that they would never be immoral, and others testify with conviction that they would never deny their testimonies of Christ and his gospel; and yet they have gone on to do these very things.

How does Satan get people to do such serious things when they are so firm about never doing them? It's simple. In Satan's attempts to destroy the souls of men, one of his greatest tools is first getting them to violate the Word of Wisdom.

In Larry's case, Satan knew it would be almost impossible to get Larry to give up his family. So the tempter started by getting him to do something that didn't appear to be all that serious—drinking a few beers. What harm could that do? But a few beers led to many beers—and then to alcoholism. Alcohol became more important to Larry than his family.

Granted, not everyone who drinks a few beers will become an alcoholic; but none of us know who will and who will not. It is important to understand that Satan uses violation of the Word of Wisdom to get us to do things we would probably never do under normal conditions.

Every year thousands of people under the influence of alcohol and drugs commit murder. Most of these people would not ordinarily have performed such a Satan-inspired act, but because of impaired judgment they may have altered their eternal possibilities. The same eternal results may follow from the immoral acts that many people commit. Many young people lose their chastity because of impaired judgment resulting from the use of alcohol and drugs. Thousands of unwanted pregnancies follow these transgressions. Frequently these babies have brains and bodies that are permanently damaged because they have been poisoned by the alcohol or drugs in the bodies of their mothers. In many cases the sin of immorality is compounded by the horrible crime of abortion.

Satan knows what he is doing. If he can get us to do something that appears harmless, he can lead us little by little to commit greater sins.

With this in mind, it would be well for you to establish a *never* that will help you keep the other *nevers* among your personal goals: I will *never* violate the Word of Wisdom!

How Could They?

The following headline has come to be quite familiar to most of us: "Star Athlete Banned for Life Because of Repeated Drug Use."As one reads such articles, he often learns that the athlete has lost a multimillion-dollar contract because of his repeated use of drugs. Questions that naturally follow are: How could he? Why would anyone give up several million dollars for drugs or alcohol? Wouldn't that much money be enough motivation to beat the addiction?

The tragic stories of these athletes teach us what a powerful tool Satan has in drug and alcohol abuse. He would have us believe that there is no problem in using these things that the Lord has commanded us to avoid. In fact, Lucifer promises us that our problems will be solved by substance abuse. He also promises fun, popularity, glamour, and peace.

The Lord warned us of these lies over a century and a half ago: "Behold, verily, thus saith the Lord unto you: In consequence of evils and designs which do and will exist in the hearts of conspiring men in the last days, I have warned you, and forewarn you, by giving unto you this word of wisdom by revelation" (D&C 89:4).

Those who would have us purchase and use substances forbidden by the Lord are indeed conspiring men. As we read ads and watch commercials, we might ask ourselves, What is the intent of the people who produce, advertise, and sell the things forbidden by the Lord in the Word of Wisdom? No matter how many possible responses our minds may pursue, they will eventually arrive at the only clear answer—money. In their desire to make money, manufacturers and advertisers of harmful products cover the truth and lie to us.

Elder Malcolm S. Jeppsen, formerly a practicing physician, cleverly highlighted this deception: "I had my own comment printed and pasted on all cigarette advertising in the magazines of my medical office waiting room. It states: 'Many of the ads in this magazine are misleading, deceptive, and are a rip-off. For example, smoking does not make one glamorous, macho, or athletic. It does make one sick, poor, and dead.'" ("Who Is a True Friend?" *Ensign*, May 1990, pp. 44–45.)

Satan would have us believe that using drugs and alcohol will give us easy solutions to our problems. Elder Marvin J. Ashton pointed out the fallacy of such thinking when he taught: "Drugs are not a 'quick fix.' They are a quick exit through a door which too often swings only one way—toward heartache and self-destruction." ("Shake Off the Chains with Which Ye Are Bound," *Ensign*, November 1986, p. 15.)

If we ask what the Lord's intent was in giving us the Word of Wisdom, the answer will be very different from Satan's objectives. God's purpose is defined in the Word of Wisdom and this purpose will be verified for each of us as we follow that revelation. The Lord's intent is that we will have good physical and spiritual health (see D&C 89: 18–21). How much better it is to place our trust in God instead of Satan and those who serve him.

Two Hearts

The heart is one of the most important organs of the human body. It pumps blood to other organs and to the limbs, nourishing them with oxygen. If your heart does an efficient job, your body will have all the oxygen it needs. However, if your heart does not pump properly, insufficient oxygen is delivered to the various parts of your body. This lack of oxygen starves the brain and other organs, resulting in sickness and possibly even in death.

The rate at which most normal, healthy hearts pump is about 70 beats per minute. There are several things that affect one's heart rate. Of great importance is the food one eats and the liquid he drinks. These substances are absorbed into the bloodstream, affecting the functions of the brain either for good or for bad. The brain is responsible for sending the signals that cause the heart to beat. If those signals are weak, the heart beats abnormally and the oxygen going to the brain is affected in return, thus causing a double problem for the heart. Coffee, tobacco, alcohol, and drugs all have this adverse effect on the heart's pumping rate. The Lord knew these things and—for these and other wise reasons—counseled us not to use dangerous substances improperly.

Another thing that can affect the heartbeat is the condition of our bodies. We should not only keep things that are harmful from entering our bodies but also work at keeping our bodies in good operating order. This is an important part of the Word of Wisdom that is sometimes overlooked. Proper diet, rest, and physical exercise are very important to the maintenance of good health. When we neglect our bodies' well-being, our hearts are forced to work harder to supply the necessary oxygen. This neglect may not be noticed at first, but eventually it can literally wear the heart out.

To demonstrate this, let's compare the hearts of two individuals. The first heart is that of someone who eats a proper diet, gets enough rest, and also gets adequate exercise. Let's assume his heart rate is 70 beats per minute. The second person does just the opposite with regard to the care of his body. Let's assume that because of this neglect his heart rate is 80 beats per minute. Person number one's heart would beat 4,200 times in an hour (70 x 60). Person two's heart would beat 4,800 times in an hour (80 x 60). In other words, two's heart would have to beat 600 more times per hour than one's. In a twenty-four-hour period, two's heart would beat 14,400 more times than one's. In one year, two's heart would beat 5,256,000 more times than one's. Considering these numbers, it is easy to see why person two's heart might wear out faster than person one's.

However, there is a greater benefit that the Word of Wisdom affords us. It has to do with another heart—the spiritual one. Just like our physical hearts, our spiritual hearts need to be cared for with proper diet and exercise. If we neglect our spiritual hearts, they can likewise wear out and fail to work properly when we need them the most.

In this connection, the scriptures say: "Trust in the Lord with all thine heart; and lean not unto thine own understanding. In all thy ways acknowledge him, and he shall direct thy paths. Be not wise in thine own eyes: fear the Lord, and depart from evil." (Proverbs 3:5–7.)

As we give our spiritual heart to God, great blessings shall flow our way. One way we can do this is by living the Word of Wisdom. As we do this, we can reap spiritual strength and eternal blessings.

Elder George Albert Smith described the relationship between spiritual health and obedience to the Word of Wisdom in these words: "I am fully convinced that the

Lord in His mercy, when He gave us the Word of Wisdom, gave it to us, not alone that we might have health while we live in the world, but that our faith might be strengthened, that our testimony of the divinity of the mission of our Lord and Master might be increased, that thereby we might be better prepared to return to His presence when our labor here is complete" (in Conference Report, April 1907, p. 19). Taking care of both our physical and our spiritual hearts will make us wonderful tools in God's kingdom.

Ideas to Remember

1. There is never a good reason for breaking the Word of Wisdom. Every time we do we hurt ourselves physically, and more important, we hurt ourselves spiritually.
2. Don't underestimate the power of Satan to destroy our lives by tempting us to break the Word of Wisdom. Violation of the Word of Wisdom can lead us to other sins. These other sins are often much greater than the breaking of the Word of Wisdom. We must remember that any time we break a commandment of God we lose a portion of his Spirit, and that loss gives Satan room to come into our lives and exercise his influence.
3. The Lord hasn't told us all the reasons why certain things are harmful to our bodies. He has told us only that we should not use these substances because they

are not good for us. We need to have faith that the Lord has our best interests in mind when he gives a commandment. The opposite is true of Satan—he has only *his* best interest in mind when he tries to get us to break the commandments.

4. As we live the Word of Wisdom, others can be affected for good. Living the Word of Wisdom is a sign to the world of our devotion to God and his commandments. As others see us live this great commandment, they may gain a desire to live better themselves and to know more about God and his commandments. But we also must remember that our violations of the Word of Wisdom could become a stumbling block for those who have not yet accepted the restored gospel or for those who are weak in the faith.

11

Serving the Master

I'll go where you want me to go, dear Lord,
Over mountain or plain or sea;
I'll say what you want me to say, dear Lord;
I'll be what you want me to be
(Mary Brown, "I'll Go Where You Want Me
to Go," *Hymns*, no. 270).

Don't You Have Anything Better to Do?

High school had been a fun time for Richard, and it was hard for him to see it come to an end. But he was also very excited about what lay ahead. Richard had received a scholarship to the very school he wanted to attend and had been accepted into the program of his dreams. As he attended school and got involved in his studies and in the various activities on campus, all of the facets of his life seemed to fit beautifully together. His first two years of college were everything he had dreamed of. Life was wonderful.

As summer approached, one of Richard's favorite professors asked him if he would be interested in a summer job that was related to Richard's major field of study. The more he talked with the professor, the more excited Richard got. Not only was this a great job but a great chance to meet some of the people whom he considered to be the best in his chosen profession. He told the professor that he wanted the job.

Richard started his summer job with enthusiasm. That excitement didn't let up all summer. He loved his job. For that matter, he loved his life—except for a nagging feeling in the back of his mind that he couldn't shake, no matter how hard he tried.

That nagging feeling had been with him ever since he had made the decision, once and for all, that he was not going to serve a mission. He had been raised in a family that had always talked about "the day you go on your mission," but his family had seemed to accept the fact that he wasn't going to serve. What was the problem? For some reason he could not get rid of the thought that a piece of his life was missing.

It didn't really make sense. Here he was, doing everything that he had ever dreamed about, yet he wasn't satisfied. As the summer drew to a close and the nagging feeling persisted, Richard made the decision to serve a mission. He was twenty-one years old, and he was going on a mission!

Several months passed. Richard had received his call and was making the final preparations to leave. The peace that he had been searching for had finally come. He knew he was doing the right thing and could hardly wait to expand his gospel knowledge and share it with others.

One week before entering the MTC, Richard went to the store to buy his two-year supply of white shirts. As he picked up his shirts, he saw a buddy from high school. Eyeing the neat white stack, his friend chuckled, "You must have settled down more than I thought you ever would. But your wardrobe is going to be kind of boring, isn't it?"

Richard smiled back and said, "My wardrobe might be kind of boring, but my life isn't going to be. I'm going to Spain on a mission."

"Spain? On a mission? You're kidding!" his friend sputtered. "Don't you have anything better to do?"

"No, I don't have anything better to do," was Richard's quick reply. And he grinned both inside and out because he knew that he really didn't have anything better to do.

Sometimes young people allow unimportant things to come between them and a mission, yet there really is nothing better and more satisfying than serving the Lord. Missionaries have never been needed more than they are needed today. President Ezra Taft Benson declared:

Today the Church needs missionaries as never before! We are required to carry the gospel of Jesus Christ to every nation of the world. . . .

This commission to take the gospel to every nation, kindred, tongue, and people is one of the signs by which believers will recognize the nearness of the Savior's return to earth. Concerning this sign of His second coming, Jesus prophesied: "And this gospel of the kingdom shall be preached in all the world for a witness unto all nations; and then shall the end come" (Matthew 24:14).

This task will require thousands of missionaries, many more than are presently engaged in worldwide missionary service today. You are needed in the service of the Lord today as never before. (*The Teachings of Ezra Taft Benson* [Salt Lake City: Bookcraft, 1988], pp. 181–82.)

A man once stated that if there were gates at the entrance to the celestial kingdom, he wanted to be the next-to-last person through them. He then explained that he believed the last person through the gates would be the Savior, because he knew the Lord would be out gathering his flock until the final moment. Knowing that it was one of the best things he could do, this man desired to serve as a missionary in one way or another throughout his lifetime. And he knew that he would be working side by side with the Savior, who declared: "And now, behold, I say unto you, that the thing which will be of the most worth unto you will be to declare repentance unto this people, that you may bring souls unto me, that you may rest with them in the kingdom of my Father" (D&C 15:6).

What Will You Give?

In the Gospel of Matthew we read that wise men came in search of the newborn Savior: "And when they were come into the house, they saw the young child with Mary his mother, and fell down, and worshipped him: and when they had opened their treasures, they presented unto him gifts; gold, and frankincense, and myrrh" (Matthew 2:11).

If you had lived then and you knew of Jesus' birth, what gift would you have given him? Our circumstances are so different today that it's hard for us to imagine what we might have given. But an even more interesting question might be, What can I give him today?

The possibilities are endless, but one gift that would surely please the Savior is the decision to teach his gospel to others. President Spencer W. Kimball taught: "Serving a mission is like paying tithing; you're not compelled—you do it because it's right. We want to go on a mission because it's the Lord's way. The Savior didn't say, 'If it's convenient, go.' He said, 'Go ye into all the world.'" (Quoted in Rex D. Pinegar, "The Living Prophet," *Ensign,* November 1976, p. 67.)

Willingly serving the Lord on a mission is one of the greatest gifts we can give to the Savior. The following stories are just two examples of the great sacrifices that many young people are making today in order to give the gift of missionary service.

Elder Vogel was a young German convert of great faith. His dream was to go on a mission, but his parents refused to give him financial support. An American member offered to assist with his mission expenses, and Elder Vogel gratefully accepted the offer. He served faithfully for a year and a half without financial worries. But one day those worries surfaced and threatened to cut his mission short. He received a letter from the wife of his sponsor, informing him that her husband had been killed in an automobile accident and that it would be impossible for her to send any more money.

Elder Vogel kept his disappointment hidden and prayed earnestly for a solution. As he and his companion, Elder Smith, passed a hospital one day, a solution to his financial problems took shape in his mind. The next day Elder Vogel made an excuse to Elder Smith and then left for a time. When he came back, Elder Vogel said little but went to bed early. A few days later Elder Smith remarked on the small bandage on the arm of his German companion, but his comment was passed off lightly.

Time passed and Elder Smith became increasingly suspicious of the periodic disappearances and bandagings until one day, unable to keep his secret any longer, Elder Vogel told him: "You see, my friend in America is dead and can no longer give support to my mission. My parents are still unwilling to help me, so I visit the blood bank at the hospital so I can finish my mission." (See Spencer W. Kimball, Conference Report, October 1971, pp. 155–56.)

A similar story was related by President Thomas S. Monson:

> I mention Jose Garcia from Old Mexico. Born in poverty but nurtured in faith, Jose prepared for a mission call. I was present the day his recommendation was received. There appeared the statement: "Brother Garcia will serve at great sacrifice to his family, for he is the means of much of the family support. He has but one possession—a treasured stamp collection—which he is willing to sell, if necessary, to help finance his mission."
>
> President Kimball listened attentively as this statement was read to him, and then he responded: "Have him sell his stamp collection. Such sacrifice will be to him a blessing." Then, with a twinkle in his eye and a smile on his face, this

loving prophet said, "Each month at Church headquarters we receive thousands of letters from all parts of the world. See that we save these stamps and provide them to Jose at the conclusion of his mission. He will have, without cost, the finest stamp collection of any young man in Mexico." (In Conference Report, October 1978, p. 83.)

Throughout our lives there will be many opportunities for us to give gifts to Heavenly Father and Jesus. As those opportunities come, remember that Heavenly Father and Jesus have given us the opportunity to receive the greatest gift of all—the gift of eternal life.

You Never Know

For many generations in the little village of Scheveningen, Netherlands, life has revolved around the fishing industry. Many of the men of the village have also been involved in the voluntary, but hazardous, task of lifesaving. Their challenge has been to save men from fishing boats that run into difficulties during high winds. Many men over the years have lost their lives at sea during these hazardous winds.

During one of these storms, a fishing boat was in distress and a rowing lifeboat went out to rescue the crew. The waves were enormous, and each of the men at the oars had to use all of his strength in order to reach the sinking vessel.

The rescue crew finally reached the wrecked ship, but their rowboat was too small to take all the men back to shore. One man would have to stay behind because the increased risk to the rescue boat was just too great.

When the rescuers made it back to the beach, they found that hundreds of people had gathered there. They held torches to guide the returning sailors through the stormy night. The original rescue crew could not go back for the last man because they were exhausted from battling the high waves and wind, so the captain of the coast guard asked for volunteers from among the people on the beach. One of those who stepped forward was a nineteen-year-old boy named Hans. As he stepped forward and heartily volunteered, his mother protested: "Hans, please don't go. Your father died at sea when you were four years old, and your older brother Pete has been reported missing at sea for more than three months now. You are the only son left to me!"

Hans's reply to his mother was, "Mom, I feel I have to do it. It is my duty." With this he left his tearful mother on the shore and disappeared into the stormy night.

The rescue boat was gone for more than an hour, before it was again sighted by those on the shore. As the boat approached the shore, the captain of the coast guard shouted to the rescuers, "Did you save him?"

The crowd on shore then saw the figure of Hans standing in the boat as he shouted the reply, "Yes! And tell Mother it is my brother Pete!" (See Conference Report, Jacob de Jager, October 1976, p. 81.)

We never know whose life may be touched or changed by what we say or do. Some of the greatest missionary work is done through the example we set for those around us. Just as Hans was willing to serve his fellowmen at great personal risk, we too should be willing to give our lives in the service of our fellowmen. As we make ourselves available to the Lord, he will direct us to those who need us the most. It would also be well for us to remember that when we refuse to serve or accept calls from the Lord we lose out on the blessings that would have been ours.

Power to Hear

It sometimes takes a great deal of courage to share the gospel with those around us. A number of years ago there was a group of Latter-day Saint teenagers in Arizona who had the courage to do what they knew was right. Most of them attended the same high school, where they made up only a handful of the total student body. They kept close to each other, yet tried to befriend those around them.

One of those whom they befriended was a girl who was deaf and had a heart defect. The only way she could know what was being said was to watch the speaker's lips. She worked hard at being a good student, but because of her two handicaps it was hard for her to get involved in extracurricular activities.

The Latter-day Saint teenagers were friendly to her and invited her to be part of their group. It wasn't long before she sought her parents' permission to receive the missionary lessons. She believed these new teachings and accepted the invitation to be baptized.

The bishop of her new ward came with her Latter-day Saint friends to the baptism. She was baptized and confirmed by the local full-time missionaries, and her new bishop stood in the circle to assist with the confirmation.

The bishop listened carefully to the words of the confirmation prayer. He was aware that she wouldn't be able to see the lips of the one confirming her, and he wanted to be able to tell her what had been said.

After the missionary confirmed her a member of the Church, he began to pronounce promises that were unusual. The bishop found himself somewhat uneasy with the words being spoken. However, as the blessing continued, the bishop felt a peace come over him. Later he invited the new convert to his office and said, "I want to tell you of the blessing the elder gave you. It was tremendous."

She paused, and with moistened eyes said, "Bishop, I *heard* the blessing."

Through the power of the priesthood she had been healed. Her hearing was fine and her heart was beating normally. This great blessing had come to her because committed and courageous young followers of Christ were willing to befriend and guide one who was in need. (See H. Burke Peterson, "The Ministry of the Aaronic Priesthood Holder," *Ensign* November 1981, pp. 35–36.)

Some of the greatest missionary work we will ever do will be accomplished in our everyday living. That is why David O. McKay gave the charge "Every member a missionary!" If we all live as Christ lived, we can be instruments in helping countless individuals receive the blessings of the gospel. As we learn to listen to the whisperings of the Holy Ghost, there will be times when he will prompt us to reach out to someone whom the Lord has prepared to receive the gospel.

Be Not Discouraged

Roger and Mark had been close friends from the first time they met each other in the seventh grade. It was hard for them to believe that they were both getting ready to serve missions. Roger was five months older than Mark and received his mission call before Mark could even turn in his application papers. Roger's call was to the Philippines, and he had a three-month wait before his departure. As the three months drew to a close, Roger confided to Mark how hard it had been for him during that time. It just seemed he had been tempted and tested in ways he had never expected.

One day as the two friends were talking, Roger reminded Mark of this struggle and warned him of what might happen when Mark received his call. At the time Mark thought to himself, *That won't happen to me. I'm stronger than Roger.*

A few weeks later, Mark's call arrived. He had two months before he was to report to the MTC. He was going to school and would take his finals the week before leaving on his mission. He knew the time would pass quickly because he was so busy with school and work.

Then it happened. As his departure date drew closer, Mark found himself becoming very discouraged. He had his wisdom teeth removed and did not recover as quickly as he thought he should. Even though he didn't feel good, he still had to finish school and take his finals. All of this seemed to bring a feeling of gloom and despair. He became irritable with his family and especially with his mother. It seemed that every day he became more discouraged and depressed.

Finally, Mark started to wonder if he should go on a

mission. As he hit this all-time low, Roger's words came ringing back to him. Roger was right, and now Mark knew the reality of Roger's warning. The next few days found Mark on his knees often, asking Heavenly Father to help him pull through this hard time. As he prayed, the answer came clearly that he *should* serve a mission and that his mission would be a very successful one. Mark also realized that Satan was mindful of this and that the devil was the source of his discouragement. This new insight and assurance helped Mark through this difficult period. Now he felt the positive influence of the Holy Ghost and could serve a successful mission.

Mark learned an important principle that we need to remember as we commit to do missionary work. Satan does not want us to help others find the gospel. Even more important, he does not want us to help others change from his ways to the ways of the Lord. Because of this, Satan will try to throw roadblocks in our way. It is important that we recognize what he is doing and refuse to let these roadblocks stop us. With the Lord's help, we can move Satan's roadblocks or find a way around them. We can then become sources of help and comfort to others as we teach them the gospel.

Ideas to Remember

1. Remember that what you do speaks louder than what you say. The most effective way to be a missionary is to

live a Christlike life. As people see how you live, they will start to ask questions and will want to know what makes you different.

2. If you don't have a desire to serve a mission, then pray for the desire to serve. Heavenly Father will help you get that desire. Once you have the desire, you can then pray to know how to best serve him and whom you should teach.

3. Satan does not want us to teach the gospel to others. He will do everything he can to stop us from helping others find the Lord. Heavenly Father, on the other hand, will do everything he can to help us proclaim his gospel.

4. Prepare now for the future. Listen closely to the Spirit and to the leaders of the Church concerning what you need to do to prepare to serve the Lord.

12

Honoring Divine Power

Apostles of a former day
To modern prophets came;
They brought the priesthood of our Lord
To bless the earth again.
The pow'rs of heav'n are opened wide
To men of God below;
The knowledge, gifts, and keys are ours,
All blessings to bestow.
(Adapted by G. William Richards,
"'Twas Witnessed in the Morning Sky,"
Hymns, no. 12.)

Lessons on the Priesthood

Just two weeks after Alan received the Aaronic Priesthood, he learned his first lesson on the importance of that priesthood. He was sitting on the front row, waiting to pass the sacrament, when he and some of the other deacons started poking each other, laughing, flipping rubber bands, and making a general nuisance of themselves. Alan's dad watched from several benches back, and it didn't take long before he decided that he needed to teach his son a lesson. He quietly walked up the aisle, grabbed Alan and one of his friends by their ears, and escorted them down the aisle toward the door. As they walked down the aisle on tiptoe, Alan noticed a red-faced lady and realized it was his mother. He had never seen her look this way before. It was not the kind of look you see on a mother's face when she is proud of her son.

When the trio got to the foyer, Alan's dad told him that if he wanted to act like a child he would treat him like one. He put Alan over his knee and gave him a spanking. Alan's friend thought sure he would be next, but instead he was told that his father would be informed if such mischief ever happened again. Alan's dad then concluded this foyer lesson with the advice that if the two boys were going to participate in priesthood duties they should do so with honor and dignity.

Alan remembered this lesson well until he was ordained a teacher. As a teacher he had the responsibility of preparing the sacrament before the Sunday meetings.

One day while he was filling the water trays, another teacher came in and threw some water in his face. Alan immediately threw a cup of water back at him.

With this, war began. The other boy squirted Alan with the little hose they used to fill the cups, and then ran. Alan filled a small bucket with water and went after him. As the other boy tried to open a door to escape, Alan let the water go. The target ducked just at the right instant—a counselor from another ward's bishopric walked directly into the airborne stream, which hit him right in the face.

Alan just stood looking in total shock. As the water ran down the counselor's face, he grabbed Alan by the arm and escorted him to the bishop's office. The bishop, in turn, marched him to his dad. When Alan's dad learned what had happened, Alan saw a look of disappointment and hurt on his dad's face that he would never forget. Alan again resolved to honor the priesthood.

However, the lesson that really taught Alan what the priesthood was all about came from a man whose name was Pete. Pete had been Alan's deacons quorum adviser and had shown a lot of love and concern for him. But Pete was elderly and crippled now. He had to use two canes to walk and was constantly in pain.

One Sunday Alan was the only priest at the sacrament table. Seeing this, Pete hobbled up to the table to assist him. Alan said the blessing on the bread perfectly, reading the words from a card. He had always been proud of the fact that he could say the prayer with such precision.

Then a great lesson on honoring the priesthood was taught to Alan by his elderly companion at the sacrament table. As Pete knelt to bless the water, he struggled in pain to get his legs to bend so that he could get down on both knees. Many of the priests had knelt on only one knee, but it was obvious Pete had made up *his* mind that if he was going to use the priesthood, he was going to use it right. When Pete was ready to begin, Alan handed him the prayer card. Pete said, "Thank you," and then set the card aside. Alan listened as Pete spoke the prayer from his heart rather than from a card.

Alan would never forget the stillness that settled over the congregation as Pete said that prayer. The Holy Ghost descended on the people there that day, and many were moved to tears. Pete said the same words that had always been said, but the difference was that he really spoke to Heavenly Father. Alan noticed that the whole congregation worshipped during the passing of the sacrament that day like never before.

Alan was never able to kneel at the sacrament table after that experience without remembering Pete and his reverence for the priesthood. Alan learned that day that when we honor the priesthood we help not only ourselves but many others as well.

"Something Special"

Roger Smith was in the middle of a typical Saturday afternoon when the phone rang. When he answered it he heard a man from a local radio station tell him that his name had just been chosen in a random drawing; if Roger answered a question correctly, he would receive a brand-new sportscar. Roger answered the question and won the prize.

Word of Roger's new car spread quickly. A member of his ward called their bishop and told him what had happened. The bishop's mind flashed back to when he was a youth. He pondered how such a car might have influenced him. As he thought about this, he became concerned that winning this dazzling prize might lead Roger away from the things that really matter most.

The next morning in Roger's priesthood meeting, one of the adults announced that something special had happened to Roger and asked him to tell about it. Roger stood up and much to everyone's surprise said, "Yes, something special did happen to me. A week ago today I was ordained a priest." Then he sat down.

During a devotional in seminary the next week, a student who was a convert to the Church mentioned how Roger's statement in priesthood meeting had affected him: "Maybe Roger was somewhat embarrassed and didn't want to mention the car. He may have been put on the spot. But he gave us a profound truth we should never forget. No worldly possession can in any way compare to the great honor and blessing of holding the priesthood of God."

Roger's bishop was still concerned about the effect the car might have on him, but his fears were calmed when he met Roger at church the following Sunday. He went up to him and said, "Hi, Roger. I'll bet you're getting a lot of phone calls from the girls at school."

"No, not so many," he responded, "but a lot from the boys."

"What do they say?" the bishop asked.

Roger replied, "They ask me when I am going to take them for a ride in my new car, and I tell them I'm not going to because I'm not going to take the car."

"You're not?" The bishop could hardly believe his ears. "How come?"

Roger answered, "Because I'm going on a mission. They told me I could take $8,000 cash instead of the car. I'm going to pay my tithing on it and then put the rest away for my mission."

The bishop later called Roger's parents to tell them how proud he was of their son. The bishop asked about Roger's reaction when he first realized that he had won a car. The bishop had visions of Roger letting out a yell of worldly ecstasy. His mother told the bishop that Roger's first reaction was, "Now my mission is paid for, but how do you tithe a car?" (See Victor L. Brown, *New Era,* July 1975, p. 5.)

It's obvious that Roger understood what a great blessing it is to hold the priesthood. Honoring the priesthood was first and foremost in his life. Sometimes it takes courage for a young man to put priesthood service first in his life. When such courage is required, he needs to have already decided what he will do. There is no question that Roger had decided before winning the car that being ordained a priest was one of the most important things that had ever happened in his life. He knew immediately what he would do with the car. Roger's priorities were in the proper order, and his priesthood would remain active and powerful.

Courageous Youth

Honoring and magnifying the priesthood takes courage and strength of character. Those who exhibit such traits will always be rewarded with the blessings that only the priesthood can afford. A great example of such courage unfolded in 1844 in Nauvoo, Illinois.

Several men were plotting the death of the Prophet Joseph Smith. Secret meetings were held, and two young men, Dennison Harris and Robert Scott, were invited to attend such a gathering at the home of William Law. Dennison's father, Emer Harris, had also been invited, but he went instead to Joseph Smith and asked him what they should do. The Prophet advised the older Harris not to go but to have the young men attend the meeting and report back to Joseph on the proceedings.

As they attended the first meeting, the boys learned of the group's conviction that Joseph was a fallen prophet and should be destroyed. Dennison and Robert reported to the Prophet what they saw and heard. Joseph asked them to attend the next meeting and again let him know of any developments.

They did as the Prophet instructed and reported to him the group's latest plans. They also told Joseph of a third meeting that was to be held the following week. He again asked them to attend and told them that this would be their last meeting. Warning them of the danger they were in, the Prophet also counseled them not to make any covenants or promises. He then gave the young men a blessing by the power of the priesthood and promised them that if their lives were taken they would receive a great reward.

Dennison and Robert attended the next meeting and listened carefully to the plans that were being laid to kill the Prophet. After the scheme had been finalized, each person was asked to take an oath of secrecy. Each did so, until only Robert and Dennison were left. They were told by the group that if they did not take the oath they would be killed. They followed the Prophet's counsel and courageously refused to take the oath.

Knives were drawn and the young men began to be forced down into the basement. However, some of the plotters protested this action. These men thought it unwise to kill the boys, because their parents would wonder what had happened and investigate. This could lead to the discovery of the plot to kill Joseph. An argument raged between the two sides until a compromise was reached. The plotters decided to threaten to kill the two if they revealed any of the murderous plans.

Dennison and Robert were released but ignored the threat, went to Joseph, and told him everything that had happened. The Prophet warned them that for their own safety they must not tell anyone about the meetings for at least twenty years. Thirty-seven years later, Dennison Harris—by then a bishop in southern Utah—finally revealed the details of this thrilling story. (See Dallin H. Oaks, "Priesthood Blessings," *Ensign,* May 1987, pp. 38–39.)

The dedication and courage of these two young men is a powerful example for all of us. We too must stand true to the priesthood and to those who hold it. There may be times when we are with people who are criticizing or making light of Church leaders. It takes courage not to join in with the criticism. It takes even more fortitude to defend the one being attacked. As we stand true to the priesthood and to God's authorized servants, great blessings will be ours.

Ideas to Remember

1. When we honor the priesthood, we help not only ourselves but other people as well.

2. If we properly align our priorities, the priesthood will remain an active force for good in our lives.

3. Every young man can be lifted beyond his natural capabilities as he uses priesthood power to serve others.

4. We must stand true to the priesthood and to those who hold it. It won't be easy, but great blessings will come to those who have the courage to honor the priesthood and defend the Lord's servants.

13

Preparing for a Celestial Marriage

While I am in my early years,
I'll prepare most carefully,
So I can marry in God's temple for eternity
(Ruth M. Gardner, "Families Can Be
Together Forever," *Hymns,* no. 300).

The Most Important Things We Ever Do

Elder Bruce R. McConkie said that the two most important things a Latter-day Saint can do in this life are to marry the right person in one of God's holy temples and then keep the covenant that accompanies this sacred marriage ceremony (see *Mormon Doctrine*, 2d ed. [Salt Lake City: Bookcraft, 1966], p. 118).

In a recent survey, 94 percent of the teenagers questioned did not understand why temple marriage is so important—why it is necessary for exaltation in the celestial kingdom. (The terms *exaltation* and *eternal life* refer to our potential to become like our Father or Mother in Heaven; when men and women are exalted, receiving eternal life, they eventually become gods themselves.)

To understand why temple marriage is necessary for godhood, please think through the following ideas:

1. If you have an eternal mate (that is, if you enter into and keep the temple marriage covenant), you will be able to have spirit children.
2. If you can have spirit children, you will have children of your own to love and to help to grow toward eternal life as our Father in Heaven loves and helps us. (See D&C 132:15–25.)

Because of the importance of temple marriage, Satan is doing everything in his power to keep you from making the proper decision about marriage. It will take real effort on your part to counteract his influence.

It is critical that you marry in the temple, and it is important that you prepare yourself so that you are ready to make and keep the special covenants that are made there. Wanting to marry in the temple is not enough. Many young people who want to marry in the temple end up settling for a civil marriage. The reason is often that by the time their wedding date arrives these couples are not worthy to enter the temple.

In the section on chastity, we discussed the "price tags" that are attached to anything of true worth. The number one price tag attached to temple marriage is chastity. Among the other things we need to do in order to enter the temple are the following:

1. Pay an honest tithing.
2. Keep the Word of Wisdom.
3. Attend sacrament meeting and other Church meetings.
4. Accept and support local and general Church leaders.
5. Try to obey all the laws and commandments of the gospel.
6. Be willing to serve and help the kingdom of God to grow.

As you prepare yourself for the temple, it may be helpful to keep in mind that it is not the bishop or the branch president that you are trying to please but the Lord. You should want to live in such a way that you can know that you are worthy in the eyes of your Father in Heaven.

Having regular interviews with your Heavenly Father can help you become worthy in his sight. This is done by asking him in prayer what you can do to prepare yourself for the temple and for the covenants you will make there.

After you ask this question, it is important to stop and wait for the answer. If you are sincere, ideas may come into your mind. You may feel that you need to quit dating a certain person, be more consistent in paying your tithing, or read the scriptures more often. Once you know what the Lord wants you to do, you can then commit to him that you will do these things and ask him for his help.

There are several factors that seem to affect whether or not a person marries in the temple and then enjoys a successful marriage. Some of these factors will be discussed in the pages ahead.

Temple Wedding or Celestial Marriage?

Several years ago a twenty-year-old girl named Susan was married in the temple. Her story is a common one and will probably sound familiar to you.

Susan had started dating Brett several months before their wedding. He was twenty-two years old, good looking, attentive and considerate—and inactive in the Church. As the months passed, their relationship became more and more serious. One night, after an especially enjoyable date, Brett pulled a ring out of his pocket and asked Susan to marry him.

But Susan had always wanted to marry in the temple. She had set that as a goal before she was even in her teens and had promised herself that she would not marry anywhere else. Susan had known that she and

Brett were getting more and more serious, but she had refused to face the possibility that he would eventually ask her to marry him. Let's face it—Susan was emotionally involved in a *big* way.

When Brett asked her to marry him, she realized that no matter how much she felt she loved him she could not marry him outside of the temple. Her lifelong goal meant too much to her. She told Brett that she really loved him and wanted to marry him, but he would have to become active in the Church and make himself worthy of a temple recommend.

Because Brett really wanted to marry Susan, he went through the motions of activity in the Church. He attended meetings, paid tithing, said he was keeping the Word of Wisdom, and did the other things his bishop said that he must do in order to receive a recommend. The problem was that Brett did all of these things just to win over Susan, not for the Lord or for himself.

Before we go any further with this story, it would be good to ask yourself a few questions: How long do you think Brett will live the gospel after he and Susan are married? Does Brett have a testimony or a desire to serve the Lord? What is wrong with the goal that Susan set for herself?

Now, back to our story. Within a few months, Brett had met the minimum requirements for a temple recommend. Susan was happy and excited. She felt that her lifelong dream was finally going to come true.

On a beautiful spring morning in June, Susan and Brett knelt at a temple altar and were sealed as husband and wife. Seven days later Brett removed his temple garment, the symbol of his sacred covenants with the Lord, and said that he was through living "the religious life." He quit attending church, no longer paid tithing, and told Susan that he had never really stopped smoking and drinking.

Susan was devastated. She could not understand what

had gone wrong. Hadn't she done what she was supposed to do? Hadn't she insisted on a temple marriage?

Within two months the couple had separated, and Susan had filed for divorce. Her "eternal marriage" had not even lasted a year. Shortly after she filed for divorce, Susan was informed that she was pregnant. Now she faced the added burden of raising a child without the help of a husband.

One of the problems that led to this unhappy situation was that Susan had the wrong goal. Susan's goal was to be married in the temple. She wanted a temple wedding. Having this goal is better than having no goal at all, but a temple wedding is simply an event. It takes place at a given hour on a given day, and then it is over. Too many teenagers choose a temple wedding as their goal.

A better and more meaningful goal than a temple wedding is the goal of having a celestial marriage. Celestial marriage is a process that begins with a temple wedding and continues day after day as a man and a woman grow together spiritually. When you have a celestial marriage as your goal, you look for more than just someone who will marry you in the temple, someone who can meet the minimum requirements. You look instead for someone who is committed to the Lord and wants to live the gospel for the rest of his or her life. You look for someone who is going to the temple for his or her own spiritual growth and for the Lord, not simply to satisfy you.

During your teen years, it is not as important to *find* the right person as it is to work on *becoming* the right person for someone else. As you become more obedient and prayerful, you increase your chances of attracting someone with these same qualities.

Once two people are married in the temple, they both need to keep the commandments so that the Holy Ghost can seal their marriage. A marriage becomes eternal not only by the power of the priesthood but also through the faithfulness of the married couple. This is another reason why it is so important to marry a person who is totally committed to living the gospel and serving the Lord.

Take Out Insurance

We have discussed the importance of developing spiritual strength and making sure that you marry someone who is dedicated to the Lord. Even if these things are in place, it is still wise to take out a little "insurance." The following story illustrates the importance of taking out marriage insurance.

Allan had been dating Jeani for several months when he realized that he was deeply in love with her. He liked the way she looked and the fun personality she had, and most of all he liked her commitment to the gospel. He finally got up enough courage to ask her to marry him. Much to his surprise, she said yes.

About two weeks later, a young woman named Cheryl called Allan on the phone. He had met her in Australia when he served there on a mission. He had really liked her but had never shared his feelings with her. She must have liked him too, because she had come twelve thousand miles to see him. Some of Cheryl's close friends told Allan that she had come to America hoping that she and Allan would marry.

When Allan saw Cheryl, his heart started to beat a little faster, and he realized that he still liked her a lot—

maybe even loved her! He knew that this was not the way an engaged man was supposed to feel about another woman, and he felt very confused. Allan then realized something that he had never even considered before. He realized that it is possible to love more than one person and, even worse, to love them at the same time. Both Jeani and Cheryl were religious, pretty, and talented, and—most confusing of all—they both wanted to marry him. In just a few weeks, Allan had gone from no potential marriage partners to two.

Allan asked himself a lot of questions: What if Cheryl had come a few months later—after I had married Jeani? Would I still have had these feelings? Would I still have struggled with the same doubts? Allan felt deep guilt because he was engaged to Jeani and yet had strong feelings for Cheryl as well.

What would you have done? Allan decided that it wasn't fair to Jeani or Cheryl—or to himself—not to be sure about something as important as marriage. After many hours of nerve-racking analysis of his situation, Allan made the decision to break his engagement with Jeani. He knew that it would be difficult for him and embarrassing for her, but he couldn't go through the rest of his life wondering if he had made a mistake.

That night after a movie, he explained his dilemma to Jeani. He told her that he felt that they should break their engagement until he was sure what he should do.

Jeani looked at him in total disbelief for what seemed like several minutes but was probably only a few seconds. She then said, "If you were not sure what you should do, why did you ask me to marry you in the first place?" Allan had just started to splutter an excuse when Jeani looked at him straight in the eye and said, "Didn't you ask Heavenly Father about our marriage before you asked me?"

Now Allan really stammered and spluttered. Finally he admitted that he hadn't prayed about it. After all, he had felt that they were in love. Wasn't that all that was necessary?

Jeani told Allan that she *had* prayed about marrying him and had received an answer before he ever proposed to her. She then told him that he had better start praying, because she was only going to give him two weeks to make his decision.

Over the next two weeks, Allan dated Cheryl almost every night; but he only got more confused. He knew that he had to make a decision and finally realized that the decision was too important to make without the help of the Lord. At last he did what he should have done earlier—he made his marriage decision a matter of prayer.

Allan did not get his answer the first time he prayed, but as the end of the two-week grace period rushed closer and closer his prayers became more and more sincere. One afternoon Allan found a quiet place, knelt down in true humility, and desperately poured out his heart to his Heavenly Father. The Lord recognized Allan's desires and needs, and before Allan got up off his knees his prayer had been answered. Although it's difficult for Allan to explain how the answer came, he knew without any doubt that he should marry Jeani. The answer was accompanied with such a feeling of peace that Allan was positive that he was making the correct choice.

That night as Allan explained his feelings to Cheryl, she told him that she had received the same answer during her morning prayer. Both of them realized that the Lord was looking out for them and helping them make the right decision.

Jeani and Allan were soon married in the Salt Lake Temple, and they have never had a doubt or a negative thought about their marriage. They have always been grateful for the assurance they received from the Lord. This knowledge has brought a sense of confidence and stability to their marriage that could not have come in any other way.

As we consider this story, it's easy to see that it would be foolish for any of us to make a marriage decision without praying about it. When "in love," a person is so emotionally involved that the person needs the Lord's help to make sure that he or she is doing the right thing. Each person is unique and has so many individual needs, desires, and characteristics; only Heavenly Father knows whether or not two people will be good for each other. He not only knows, but also can help the couple know as well. And in order for them to know, they need to ask him.

Referring to the important decision of whom to marry, President Kimball counseled, "The decision is not made on the spur of the moment. It is something you plan all your life. Certainly the most careful planning and thinking and praying and fasting should be done to be sure that of all decisions, this one is not wrong." (*The Teachings of Spencer W. Kimball*, ed. Edward L. Kimball [Salt Lake City: Bookcraft, 1982], pp. 301–2.)

A positive answer to prayer ensures that your marriage *can* be successful. It does not ensure that it *will* be successful. Once a couple is married, each partner must continue to grow spiritually and to show love, understanding, and unselfishness if the marriage is to succeed.

Ideas to Remember

1. The two most important things you will ever do in this life are to marry a righteous person in the temple and then keep the covenant you make there.

2. The temple marriage ceremony is the "godhood ordinance." You need an eternal mate in order to have spirit children and become like our Father or Mother in Heaven.

3. Because of the importance of temple marriage, Satan is doing everything he can to keep you from this eternal blessing.

4. Wanting to marry in the temple is not enough. It will take real effort on your part to counteract Satan's influence.

5. We can have personal interviews with the Lord by asking him in prayer what we need to do to grow in spiritual strength and then committing to do the things that the Holy Ghost brings to our minds.

6. A better and more meaningful goal than a temple wedding is a celestial marriage. Celestial marriage is a process that begins with a temple wedding and continues day after day as a man and a woman grow together spiritually.

7. You need to marry someone who is going to the temple not just to please you but because he or she is committed to the Lord and wants to live the gospel throughout this life and forever.

8. During your teen years, it is more important to *become* the right person than to *find* the right person.

9. When a person is in love, he is so emotionally involved that he needs the Lord's help to make sure that he is doing the right thing. Each person is unique

and has so many individual needs, desires, and characteristics that only Heavenly Father can tell whether or not two people will be good for each other.

10. Prayer only ensures that a marriage *can* be successful, not that it *will* be. Each partner must continue to grow spiritually and to show love, understanding, and unselfishness if the marriage is to succeed.

Index